Ninna Kiel Nielsen

WIPE YOUR SLATE!

Layout and cover design:
Stefan Kiel Nielsen

Translated from "Ryd Dig Op" by
Brigit O'Connell

First edition, May 2015

ISBN-13: 978-87-996611-1-4
ISBN-10: 87-996611-1-X

Publishing:
Amuse A Muse

Contents

WIPE YOUR SLATE!

My thanks...

A big thank you to my sweet and funny son, who, with his fantastic as well as odd and quirky sense of humour, has supported, criticised, pushed and forced me through this process. Stefan, you are a brilliant sparring partner.

Also a big thank you to my long time friend Brigit O'Connell, who volunteered to translate this whole thing into understandable English – and never knew what hit her! I know, that is has been a challange to make it my words, and I am forever in debt to you – which I dont mind!

Cleaning up your 'stuff' and your finances will calm your mind, and set you free

to concentrate on what you really want to do so you can reach your aimed for goals

WIPE YOUR SLATE!

Let me introduce myself.

I am neither a life coach nor a psychologist, but I have written this book, because I have gone through a process, that I didn't recognize as such until I was almost half way through. I want to share my experience with everybody who may be in a similar situation.

This is not a self help book. It won't teach you to visualize success while sitting on your couch. There are no tests with answer sheets. It is a book outlining my experience of the chain reaction started by doing 'something', and ending with good results. You get peace in your life by cleaning up in your own 'shop', and come to realize what you actually need and like.

There are challenges posed by a project like this, and there will be further challenges, even when you have achieved the result you wanted. Because then, there will be no excuses left for not acting on all the ideas that have been buzzing around in your head, but couldn't break free because you were too busy living the way you do now.

Most live our lives covered by a thick blanket of unreality hiding what is important for us, because we have never consciously made up our minds about what our personal values are. Once you know what you stand for, you can make life a lot easier for yourself. So why not find out what your honest deep values are, and perhaps make life simpler and easier for yourself – a better quality life.

This is a book meant to challenge. A book to inspire or maybe challenge you to live an easier life.

Because you influence everything happening around you with:

- **the things you say;**
- **the things you do;**
- **the way you live;**
- **your home and your possessions;**
- **your finances;**
- **the people you see;**
- **the work you do; and**
- **the goals you want to reach.**

But why did I hit this "live a simple life and find out what you really need"-road?

Because I had a problem that prevented me from breaking out of a deadlock, and was in a situation that had taken all power away from me. This process sent me on a 'journey' that I hadn't foreseen, and I want to share this, because life should be lived, not fought.

So what can you do?
You can start inside your own door,
so hang on and

WIPE YOUR SLATE !

WIPE YOUR SLATE!

My story

We all have areas in our lives which pull us down. Small scale or big scale. It could be finances, family relations (I am talking negative relations), work related problems, home or possessions, but when you start cleaning up in one area, other areas will follow. When you start feeling in charge of one area that used to weigh you down, you gain the power to go further. One action sets in motion another action.

A hoarder was created.

My problem was things. Lots and lots of things. I 'drowned' in my possessions. I was choking! Physically and mentally, because I had kept everything I had been given and acquired, without questioning any of it. I carried too much of the past, and was living so much in the future (read: planning what I should do when I got the time) that I forgot to be in the present.

It started when I was a child.

> I was 7 years old. It was my mother's birthday, and she had
> invited all her girlfriends for coffee. One of them brought
> a very special gift for me. A little pink and gold coffee cup
> filled with chocolate caramels wrapped in tulle and closed
> with a big bow. It was so little-girl-pretty, and I was excited!
> It went right up on my shelf – together with another small
> cup which my mother found in her cabinet. It was a cup that
> had been given to her, when she was a child. A white and
> cold cup with "The Sweet Girl" written on it.
> During the following 6 month period of one Christmas,
> one Easter, and my own birthday, it became apparent to
> everybody who visited us that I collected small coffee cups,
> so the collection kept growing, and before the story about
> my collection mania had been 'killed', I was the owner of 26
> different cups! Eight years old!
> Eventually, I got tired of dusting the cups and keeping my
> friends from touching them, and told my mother that I would
> rather not have the cups sitting out in the open anymore. My
> mother didn't know that her answer would make a lasting
> impression on me. She said:" But Darling, what do you think
> all the nice people who have given you the cups will think
> when they come here and see that you didn't appreciate
> them?

But I did appreciate them! And I didn't want to make anyone sad
or disappointed over having given me something, that I just wanted
to put in a box in the basement making me look ungrateful. I

wasn't ungrateful. I was just a little girl, who didn't like dusting, and who certainly had never planned to collect coffee cups. That episode gave birth to my hoarder trait.

GUILTY conscience

I am absolutely sure my mother didn't intend this, but the effect was that for too many years I kept gift that I

hadn't wanted;

didn't want to use or display; and

didn't have the heart to return, for fear of disappointing the person who had given it to me,

and kept things

which would only take up space in drawers and cabinets; and

which I kept moving around my house from one place to another without any joy.

The hoarder was born!

My parents and grandparents had lived through the Second World War, and that had taught them to save everything, because almost everything was in short supply, and those shortages lasted for several years after the war had ended. In those days, you knew that you would probably have a use for things which today we simply throw out. So I saw how every piece of string, every rubber band, and every piece of wrapping paper were saved. Both my mother and my grandmother ironed – yes, ironed – Christmas gift wrap, so it could be re-used the following year. Even today, I find it difficult to rip nice wrapping paper when I get a gift.

But I couldn't go on saving all these things. **Something had to happen!**

At that point, I had no idea what was weighing me down, so I ran in circles to get done all the things I thought I should do. With all the duties and obligations I had to live up to, I suffered from a permanent bout of guilty conscience. The duties took charge of me. Without being obsessive about it, I was still overwhelmed by the cleaning of my house and my things. Due to all the things I had collected, it was never done as well as I wanted it to be, because it was so time consuming. I had hundreds of projects on the go that I never finished. I could never relax, because there was always something I had to do.

I spent a lot of time looking for things that I couldn't find when I needed them. When I finally found them, either they were too small, too big, wrong, ruined, wrinkled or out of fashion. So I bought new things, nice things, cute things, modern things, but none of this changed the inner turmoil, and I bought these things in spite of not having the money to do so.

I was never at peace with myself to be in exactly the place, where I was physically. I was always planning a couple of hours, a couple of days, or a couple of weeks into the future. I became an expert in 'panic rescues' and was the owner of endless post-it reminders and to-do lists. I never enjoyed being where I was, because my thoughts were always somewhere else – far off in the future. I was not 'present'.

At some point, when the situation felt really chaotic, my son had a birthday party, and we took photos. My son also took some the next day after the clean-up, and it was before digital cameras, so I didn't see the photos until a couple of weeks later – and I had a shock. It was a wake-up call of gigantic proportions! The 'after' photos looked as if the party was still going on. Stuff everywhere. Furniture everywhere. The photos showed that I was drowning in things. It suddenly became obvious that I had collected like a pack rat. I had saved everything that I had been given or bought through all my adult life, which at that point was approximately 20 years! I had never thrown anything away. I had said yes to everything other people wanted to get rid of, and in which I could see possibilities. I had aimlessly bought things. I could furnish at least 4 family homes. I carried too much old baggage. My home didn't meet the needs for the life I lived, or rather, wanted to live.

It was a very, very tough experience for me. I, who loved magazines with photos of beautifully furnished, functional homes with quality designed furniture. I had not been able to see that I had turned my home into a storage area for both good and bad old mementos and things of different sorts and quality. Everything from small pieces furniture to books and vases. I cannot enumerate them. There was everything – I literally lived in a flea market.

I was shaken to the core, and then relief flooded me. One photo had made it clear what had happened, and it took a whole night and the next day to digest it.

Right then and there I decided that I wouldn't own more than a bed, a beautiful dining/working table, 8 comfortable chairs, 7 sets of clothes (one for each day of the week), 2 pairs of shoes, one hand bag and a really cool wristwatch!

When revelations like this occur, it is easy to become obsessed. When I realized that I had to disown what I had done all my adult life, it took a while before I found the golden mean, and the end result wasn't quite as drastic as described above, but almost. And I have to admit that those totally strict limitations still occasionally pop into my head.

When I observed my whole life from this sort of bird's eye view, and not least my everyday life, I had to admit that nobody had twisted my arm to make me live the way I had done – not even my parents or grandparents. It was all me! The small coffee cups may have been the start, just maybe, but I was the cause. Nobody forced me.

Who had collected all my belongings?
Who decided what I should do?
Who made me feel those obligations?
Who had given me the guilty conscience?

ME! – Nobody else!

It is a bit shattering to admit that I was so busy, only because I had constructed my day to day life, so as to make me feel like a bee in a bottle. That my home was furnished and decorated in a way which made it difficult to keep clean and neat. That I had made a lot of commitments, which I didn't actually have the time to fulfil, but had taken on because I am a helpful people pleasing soul, who didn't take the time to help myself. Because it is so much easier to help other people. It is always easier to see the solution to other people's problems. But I didn't realize that the bustle was just as much in my head as in my home. The anxiety I felt every time I had tried to clear some space created a noise in my head, because I was only moving things around. I never accomplished getting rid of anything, for which, in reality, I had no use. But now I understood: The noise in my head was directly related to the quantity of things I had stored in the few square meters of my home.

It was a surreal experience to stand in front of the mirror and recognize that it was my own choices, not any outside influences that had gotten me to where I was. I could only point at myself. So then the question was: How should I start changing my life? Where should I begin?

The answer came fast: I wanted to start with something that I thought I could handle. Something physical. Something visible. I would start changing my home, so I could gain some perspective and control my home environment.

"Operation Big Purge" started! I began with a really firm hand – the method is simple, it hurts, it is absolutely possible and I will write about it later – and the result is fantastic. I got so much 'air' in my surroundings that I just had to continue. I had started a physical and mental avalanche. I cleaned and cleared my home, my way of life, and as a result, my head. I found out what should fill my life, and what wasn't functioning anymore.

Today my home is the place where I get my energy, before I leave for the outside world. My home is also the place I return to at night without getting overwhelmed by all the things I must do. But when cleaning up just things could have that effect, what would happen, if I took control in other areas?

What **else** could I clean up and out?

- My finances	Where did I spend money on something which wasn't neccessary, and which didn't give me pleasure?
- My shopping habits	Did I ever think about, how much I bought that wasn't on my shopping list
- My routines	Did I do things that simply had no purpose?
- My daily life	Did I just complicate it for myself?

Yes, and **everything** was **picked up, tossed** and **turned.**

So I took apart my life and put it back together. Turned it into something much simpler, much more functional, a lot less time consuming, freer, and much more wonderful!

Now this sounds like quite a big mouthful, and it was. Because until you tear down the wall, it is difficult. But once it is down, it becomes a sport. You can 'smell blood' – or fresh morning air – your choice. And it works! Even if it just starts with a physical clean up and out of things.

A lot of crucial questions popped up. Questions I had never asked myself, because my head had no room for them, and which gave me a queasy stomach, because I had forgotten to be myself. I had forgotten to be authentic, to recognize my own values, and to live by them. It is so easy to forget to be true to oneself.

In the middle of my cleaning out I found a newspaper article I had saved for many years without ever thinking about it, but it must have 'spoken' to me at a very early stage. I just hadn't listened. It is about 'The Dream of the Empty Room'. It is all about how we cannot get enough stuff. We fill our homes with things that make us feel safe. We collect, hide and bond with everything from pots and pans to decorative objects. If there is a space on the wall, we immediately find something to fill it.

I had that confirmed a couple of years ago, when I had my kitchen completely renovated. Not because I wanted it fashionable, but because the old one was falling apart! Renovating one area invariably leads to unforeseen needs to do the same in others, so I couldn't stop at just the kitchen. I lived in an open space apartment, so when I got a new floor in the kitchen section, I also had to get one in the living room.

I decided that now everything was already a mess, I might just as well paint the living room, while nothing was in its right place anyway. It did not really need painting, but then it would be done. A lot of stuff had to go into my 12 square metre bedroom, and the things – and I – were stuck for a couple of days. Never have so many things been stored in such a small place. But I was already an expert at that. A lot of the furniture stood on end, including a big sofa, and I got a lot of exercise crawling in and out in order to find my bed.

So on a sunny Saturday I painted the living room. A good friend came over with a 'reward'-cake, and there was no space for it anywhere but in the empty room. So I set up a

*couple of chairs in front of the big window and our coffee
cups in the window sill. We talked about what a big job it
was to renovate, especially 2 rooms at the same time in a
relatively small apartment. My friend got a little absent, and
all of sudden she said: "What a wonderful peaceful room
this is! There is nothing here to disturb."*

I felt as if somebody had shaken my brains into place, because the
first thing that popped into my head was the plan I had, when I was
still living with my parents. The plan for how I would live, when I
moved out. Because in my childhood home I was surrounded by
collectors. I had had the dream about the big room with the big
window, the gigantic bed with white bed linen, a big green plant,
a telephone and a closet for my things. What else would I need?
A place with a roof, heat, a bed, and the ability to stay in contact
with family and friends. That was what I would need. The longing
had obviously been there from start. I had just chosen not to
listen to myself. I had been the nice girl, who said 'yes, thank you'
for all the things I would rather have been without. I didn't need
to own them, even if they were good things.

So while I was cleaning out, I thought about how exciting it would
be to have an empty home, walk into a room and ask oneself:
What do I really need? What does it take to make me function
optimally. Would I go straight to Ikea, to an expensive designer
store, or to a flea market to 'build a home'? Or would I just walk
in, close the door and take my time to find out, what I really
wanted, without any outside influence at all. Looking back now,
I have no doubt about what I should have done:

I would need a bed with a duvet, pillows and bed linen.

I have to have showers or baths, so I would need towels.

I have to get dressed, so I would have 7 top to toe outfits – one for each day of the week. For now, forget about fashion. We are talking bare necessities.

The next thing would be a big table with at least eight chairs – where I could work and dine with my loved ones.

I would need to cook, so a pot, a knife, some plates, glasses and cutlery – not a lot of gadgets. Just the stuff needed to create a good meal.

What comes next? A comfy chair or a sofa ... but then we already get to whether that is necessary. Comfortable yes, but necessary? Can you make do with a bed, a table and a chair? And how would that feel? Stressful or liberating?

I can only speak for myself. It would be liberating and honest.
And that was how it turned out, but only after a long fight, and
it wasn't quite as simple as described above. Very close though.

Douglas Coupland in "Generation X" expresses it like this:

**"I have the need for less in my life
Less past.
We store, save for seasons, save for
bad times, save.
We have 10.000 of square feet of
malls and shops.
Why?
How much do we need?"**

The above was written in 1991, and is more relevant than ever. We consume more than we could ever have imagined in the early '90s. We would do better to think more quality and much less quantity.

WIPE YOUR SLATE!

A Childhood Memory

In my adult life I have questioned, why I feel the need to live in a minimized environment, and today I know that it is easier for me to feel good about a few good things rather than many things. I can easily do without the quantity, which just produces confusion, noise and extra work.

This has made me think of a childhood girlfriend.

I once had quite a large extended family, who loved to give present, and since I liked dolls, I was given new ones almost every Christmas and birthday. One day my brother and I had a contest to see, if he had more model planes than I had dolls. I cannot remember who won, but I do remember that my brother's count was 40 dolls! From the 1 inch doll to the very big glass doll. All these dolls had beds and prams, clothes and accessories, so the equipment was in order.

When I was 8, my family moved to a new town and into quite a new building right next to a very old one. The old building was poorly maintained and in a very bad state. Linda lived there with her mother, father, and an older sister. We were the same age and quickly found each other in the back yard, where we played daily after school. When the weather was bad, we played at my place, because Linda didn't want me to come to her home. But I finally did, and then I understood why she hadn't wanted to bring me there. I didn't come from a wealthy background, but neither did we go without anything at home. Here, for the first time in my life, I saw a family struggling to keep things together.

Linda shared a room with her big sister, but not in quite the same nice way my brother and I did. The room was very small, and there was only space for a dresser with six drawers, a bunk bed, a small mirror, and a coat rack hanging on the door. That was all. Linda's clothes were in the two lower drawers, her sister's in the next two, and then the girls each had one drawer for their personal belongings. Only one drawer for all the personal things! Toys, poetry books, glossy pictures, dolls. Everything!

Linda had one doll, and she loved it! I didn't feel like that at all. I had dolls I didn't care about at all, and I had dolls that I liked, but I didn't love any of them.

We also played a lot with paper dolls, and they evoked the same feelings. I didn't know how many I had, but I had a lot. Linda had three. One, which was almost worn to pieces, and two that her sister had drawn for her. I understood why she appreciated the paper dolls her sister had made. They were special and made for her alone.

Today I understand that those feelings were a kind of jealousy. Jealousy over being able to appreciate one special thing. I didn't appreciate my things, because I simply had too many. Jealousy is not a nice feeling, and luckily not something from which I normally suffer, but I was jealous of Linda's serenity about having just a few things, that made her really happy. I had lots of things, which didn't mean all that much to me, because there were just too many.

When I had to set some parameters for my cleaning, the realization of where I wanted to go with my need for getting unimportant things out of my life made the memory of Linda stand out clearly. For me, wealth has nothing to do with quantity. It is all about being surrounded by things I need.

WIPE YOUR SLATE!

Enough about me – your turn!

Let us start with something common to all of us, and the most important 'thing' in the world: People.

Without other people we are nothing – no matter the relationships we have, no matter how irritating or wonderful they are, no matter if we are close or distant to each other. We mirror each other. We relate to other people's successes and failures. We see role models and the reverse. All this makes us who we are. The one most important factor in the world is the people around us.

Most of us have dreams and goals. We want to be rich, or at least have money 'enough'. Some of us want to be slimmer, others want to travel the world, we have all kinds of different wishes. But in reality, it is not about having more money, or toned bodies, or being able to go to Timbuktu on a whim. It is about how this would make us feel. The wishes are very often not in themselves goals, but the expected outcomes and how they would change our lives are.

Unfortunately, many of us have such a hodge podge of wishes that we never get close to any of them, because we don't think about what lies behind them. We let ourselves be influenced by the world around us, instead of letting us be inspired. It is fine to take a look at a neighbour's success, but that is not necessarily the way you should go. Therefore, it is important to look into why we get impressed by what happens to others. It is possible that your neighbour's success would be a disaster for you. So goals should not be copied. They have to be analyzed to produce a plan for how to reach them, and to understand what kind of feeling will result from reaching the goal.

First, some weeding is necessary. Cleaning up old perceptions, old habits, bad finances, dull job, old stuff. You should make yourself free, before you start rebuilding. By removing the excess, the not necessary, the purposeless, you can approach the core of who you are, and what you stand for. The job is to scrape away everything we don't need, until the core of our values is left. When you possess only the absolute necessities and whatever characterizes your set of values, and there isn't anything left to distract, you can start creating whatever you want.

So now you have to start 'freeing' yourself for unnecessary ballast – whatever that is. You may think: Holy Moly, that is not easy to define, but let's work on it. Actually it can be expressed in two sentences:

How do you want to live, and what will you do to achieve it?

Please note that I write 'will do', not 'can do', because everything has its price. We can achieve most things. We can move to where we want in life. But is comes with a price, and to achieve new goals you have to work, and work hard. Sometimes you have to destruct, and sometimes you have to revise and/or correct.

So describe yourself. Write down on a piece of paper how you see yourself and how you want your home to be.

Are you a career person, or a handyman – made for high heels or slippers – or a bit of everything?

Are you a person who takes a hike in the mountains or a shopping trip to a big city?

Do you prefer big family gatherings, or small intimate dinners?

Are you a creative or a practical person, or both? Are you introvert or extrovert?

Do you prefer lots of colours, or do you go for black and white minimalism?

Etc.

Ask yourself questions about the important things in your life, and then ask yourself, how they fit with the way you live. If they do, then it is perfect, congratulations! Then you are a very happy person, and you have no reason to continue reading this book. If so, give it away to a friend, who needs it. After all, you haven't managed to put dog ears on too many pages yet. But if you, like many of us, need some improvements, then read along.

You should concentrate on the things that mean the most to you. It is a process by which you first cut away, and then add back on once you find out what is missing. First you have to 'undress', and then you can make a plan for, how you 'dress'. The third thing you have to consider is how much you will do to reach your goals, and in which order this should happen.

Does this sound like a big project? It is – perhaps! It does take work, persistence and a good portion of self discipline, but it is a road you decide to walk. Start in one place and work to change the things that limit you. There are many people who dare to travel into dangerous and undiscovered places in the world. But there are even more people who do not dare to take a walk into their own lives, so if you start, you can count on getting some regular excitement. And isn't that what is so great about travelling? To experience something new and fun. Because that will also happen.

It is fun
to reach a goal.

WIPE YOUR SLATE!

Life stages

Let's see what we actually need – not to mention when we need it – because our needs change throughout our lives, and if we are wise, we change our surroundings accordingly.

Have you ever stopped to consider whether you are going in the direction, you really want to go, be that in your relationships, your home, your family, financially. Have you asked yourself whether you are happy the way things are? Whether you are on your way to get what you want? Do you need, what other people need, or do you follow the trends just to 'keep up with the Jones's? Or have you not given it any thought at all, and just done what was expected of you?

It is a challenge to define your needs! Or should I say wishes, because needs are necessities you cannot do without. A fulfilled wish is something that makes you feel good, as if being given a reward.

So what do we humans need? A lot of research has been conducted in this area, and I have just picked from the pile and chosen Maslov's pyramid of needs, which – very unscientifically – goes like this:

1 Physical needs – food, sleep, sex (think reproduction!) etc.;

2 Need for security – safety, stability, protection from inclement weather, from pain etc.;

3 Social needs – community, love, friendship and the need for connections to single individuals and groups;

4 Need for recognition – self respect, self confidence, talent, status and dignity;

5 Need for self-realization – achieve goals, acknowledge talents and skills, experience highlights;

6 Connection between the needs.

This means that the first three sets of needs have to be satisfied, in order to provide the strength to procede to the next three sets. Boring information, I know, but let's see, what we – in the western world – in 2012, apart from the above 6 points, actually need to live a normal everyday life without bigger problems. I am not thinking about the 17 year old girl who says: "I absolutely totally need that Vuitton-bag!".

We need a chair, a table, a bed, food, a roof over the head! That's it – just about! But the thing is, that when we have covered our basic needs, then we want 'more', and this 'more' differs a lot from one person to another.

Personally I always know, what I don't want. But that doesn't mean I always know what I do want. I have come far enough to know that if I am in doubt, then I don't need it, whatever it is. Actually, it can be a bit of a strange
feeling, and right after finishing my cleaning out, it felt like emptiness. Do I really need nothing? My bed is fine, I am meeting friends later in the day, my fridge is filled. But then the feeling of freedom sets in: I am not a slave of things. I can manage no matter what, because I know that I have what I need. It is pure luxury, and makes me feel so privileged.
This doesn't mean that I don't want anything, but the wish list is short. I have become fantastically/fanatically (!) selective about the stuff, I carry over my threshold, and I am ready to wait for that special thing, which feels 'right' and comes to me naturally. Another advantage of searching for the right things is that I more and more often experience that the hunt brings me into contact with people and places I don't know at all, and I get to explore things, I never before knew existed. Because I take my time. I don't have to rush, I will get it. It is not life or death, and if I don't get it now, I will survive just fine. And sometimes when I do find 'the thing', the need/wish has vanished, but the search has been fun and given me new values.

We are all different from one another. Gender, age, married or single, with or without children and so on. Each situation makes for different needs, and I will describe them below.

The different life stages have different needs:

The young person moving away from home

There are two different types of youngsters moving away from home. There are the ones, who take whatever furniture they had in their rooms, get presents from family, and buy the rest little by little. This first home very often looks exactly like what it is. Odds and ends. Cosy and familiar. The advantage is, that this home takes form slowly as new needs appear. There is a good chance this home will grow into one with personality.

The other youngsters are the ones, who go out and buy everything at once. Some have the money, some buy with credit cards, some get help from their parents. Sometimes the parents have even bought the condo. This start is not very healthy, or for that matter, very exciting, as it doesn't give the young person a realistic understanding of how to make his or her own life, and it doesn't provide the satisfaction or the joy of practicing the art of growing up. The home is often very nice, and very impersonal, because everything has been bought on 'the same day', and therefore, is probably no more than a perfect reflection of what the 'right' must-haves are right now. In addition, it will require a lot more changes over time compared to the home created on the basis of needs.

My first home was created by all the furniture I had in my room at my parents place, and even though my apartment consisted of only 42 square metres, there was a lot of space between the different pieces of furniture. I loved the idea of getting my own home, but if I were to start all over now, I would say 'no, thank you' to all the well meaning people, who had things they thought I probably needed (read the section "My Story"). You can never go wrong choosing quality, and if I had taken to heart the lesson Mrs. Gram gave me, I would have been rich now.

Mrs. Gram was the executive assistant in the office, where I was a trainee. She was a stately, well dressed lady, (I was very young, so she was probably only in her late 30s – early 40s!) a person everybody respected, and when she raised her voice, you listened and followed orders. But she was also the one, who was there to help, when something went wrong. She was a valkyrie with a heart of gold.

When I got engaged, she gave a long speech. In her opinion I got engaged too young. She also gave me a wooden tray and a mixing bowl. The tray was an original Silva tray and the bowl was a Margrethe bowl. (Danish design objects of good quality) This was in 1970, and I still have both. They still work and still look beautiful. Mrs. Gram had impeccable taste when it came to good quality functional things. My fiancé was not of the same quality (she was right about that too). I got married – and divorced!

A home should not be filled with temporary items. Better to do without. Because things that move in temporarily, become permanent fixtures. You don't get to save up for the good thing, the one you really wanted, because what you have works. Try to be brave and leave the space open until you can buy the right thing. Buying something you have been looking forward to getting is extremely satisfying.

Young people should be advised to move into their first home without too much ballast. Too often they move with way too much old stuff, because their parents think they need it, and because they, in order to avoid conflict, won't say no. Don't let that happen. Tell your kids that they can ask if they need something, and let them go with a minimum of possessions. When they have just moved out, they have better things to do than 'play house' as if they were middle aged. If they have the bed, the shelf and the dresser from the teenage room, they will be fine. The rest can come later.

They, and all the rest of us for that matter, should learn to say NO, THANK YOU, and well meaning parents must learn not to put on pressure (like "well, you might need these serving plates, and these four will be nice, when you invite friends over – and, as we all know, those dishes are exactly what you need for a pizza party). Too many young people are drowning in kitchen equipment.

Don't buy medium quality items. Medium quality can be defined as not top quality, but not cheap bargains. If you buy cheap flea market things, you can easily sell or give them away later. If you buy medium quality things, the cost will add up to a substantial amount of money, so they will be difficult to sell when your want the sale to finance the purchase of 'dream' things.

Having experienced leaving home with tons of household things and furniture, I did it differently. When my son left home, I told him that he could point out the things he wanted, but he should watch out, because he might end up getting them! Wisely, he only wanted the glass table he had claimed the right to, when he was twelve years old, and a TV bench. Then he took his own things: Bed, desk, shelf, and dresser. Whatever he might need, he would buy, as the need arose. Smart kid! But unfortunately, friends and family took 'revenge' and showered him with kitchen equipment, because such a young man would immediately start making big dinners! Yeah right! At the house warming party he got 2 stove scrapers (for a ceramic stove he had bought), 2 egg beaters, 2 mixers, and 4 salad sets, plus an impressive number of cook books, even though everybody knew that he wouldn't bother to even so much as turning on the stove. Neither did he – for years!

Singles

If you are single, you are sort of on the luxury side of things. You can do exactly what you want. You don't have to ask anybody. So build the home that matches the way you live and supports your interests. Appreciate the moment – make things as simple as possible, so you have the ultimate freedom. The less domestic duties, the better.

If being single wasn't a conscious choice, you can end up in a trap: Living in a temporary state, living 'on hold', until the 'one and only' comes and 'rescues' you. This is not acceptable. Appreciate yourself, and make yourself a beautiful home. A simple base filled with quality. You deserve to live a life just as good as anybody else's. The money will be well spent, even if your status changes to 'in a relationship'.

Minimize the material side of your life and make room for experiences and yourself. It is not the multitude of crystal in the cabinet, that makes life feel good. That happens when good wine is served in any kind of glass in the company of great people.

The Young Couple

It can be difficult to move in together, when two kinds of taste and old habits have to merge. I will take the risk of being accused of gender stereotyping and generalization and will jump in with both feet. A lot of younger women have a pronounced taste for 'cute', and 'lovely', for 'candelabra' and crystal lamps, for a 'castle' look, or what ever the trend is right now, and a lot of young men are into sports items, amplifiers, tech toys and everything that can be manipulated with a remote control.

If you have the guts, one way to handle this could be for both to part with everything they own, except personal belongings, and start all over again together. But only a few can agree on that. The advantage would be not only that you could find out, what the possibilities are, given the size of your home, but also that you get to decide together how the area will be used. Alternatively, both parties' stuff gets pushed in there, so you have two of everything in two different styles – and half the living space.

Insurmountable problems may arise. A lot of men do not get involved with decorating the home. The result is that they end up living in totally feminine environments. Some women are absolutely implacable, when it comes to letting their partner's things out in the daylight – or even through the door. But whether it is about pearls, roses and mansion atmosphere, or sports trophies, german beer mugs and remote controls, a home is meant to be for all the people living there. If you don't have room for anything as simple as each other's favourite things, how on earth will you be able to make room for each other's personalities. Personalities which should preferably produce a mutually agreed upon living environment. Unfortunately, too often the girls do want the guys, but do not want their belongings.

A couple of days after a young couple had moved in together, I was invited to come and see their new home. When I walked up the staircase, I saw a black, modern lamp (expensive brand) standing outside the door. When I came in, I made them aware that they had forgotten it outside. The temperature got a bit lower, because it hadn't been forgotten. It was put there, because the young girl "would under no

*circumstances have a lamp like that in her home". It didn't
fit her style.*

Here was a young couple, who hadn't touched upon the subject
of how their future home should look. The home was filled with
her things, and as most of his things didn't fit in, they had been
put in the basement. He wouldn't let go of the lamp, but it was
out on the staircase, and was later moved to join his other things
in the basement. She won.

*A young acquaintance , a musician (piano wonderkid) was
about to move in with his fiancée. A very, very big problem
arose. The fiancée wouldn't have his piano in their new home,
because it was too big. That relationship ended there.*

A piano is big, but it can hardly be love, if you can take your
so-called big love's passion away. A home should be designed
just like a relationship. With care, mutual respect and room to
be yourself and be together.

The young family

When children come into a family, more space is required. Well,
it takes space to house a family, but let's be honest, not that much.
These days, it seems that when you build a family, you have to have
at least twice the space you had before. But wait a moment. A
baby doesn't take up much space for quite some time, and grows
so fast that its needs change every couple of weeks.

Until children are 4 – 5 years old they want to be where their
parents are. Many parents incorrectly think that smaller children
need their own space, but that is merely the parents' needs
projected onto the children. Not many children have a need to

be alone. We put babies to sleep in their own rooms, while the nicest thing we know is to sleep close to someone! Really quite interesting. Babies are gregarious– like the rest of us. Let them stay close.

So wait making the investment in a big new house or condo. A dresser for clothes, a bed, and a space for diapers is sufficient. Of course, a small child should have the opportunity to sleep in a quiet place, and it can be nice having a separate room for a small child, but realize that having the very small baby in your bedroom provides a feeling of security. When they get older they can begin sleeping alone, so don't change everything right from day one. It is expensive to become parents, and piling on new big housing expenses, before you know your actual space requirements only adds unnecessary stress. Nothing bad will result from waiting a while.

When the day comes, and the child needs its own room, you shouldn't invest in a lot of cheap children's furniture. Buy an adult sized good quality chair. It can be used forever, and you can use at night, when baby doesn't want to sleep, or while reading for the child, when that time comes. A table of appropriate height and a couple of small chairs for the child to sit and draw and play, some shelving for toys, a bed, of course, and lots and lots of floor space completes an adequate room for a child.

Changing the topic, I have to ask: Has anybody ever considered, instead of toys, giving parents money for a child's savings account? In no time at all, a child will have 6 tonnes of toys in every con- ceivable ugly colour. Grandparents on both sides give presents, all costing a fortune, (because all kinds of toys in boxes cost a fortune) and it can add up to enormous amounts. Add to that gifts from the rest of the family, friends and others. Kids are drowning in toys that hold their interest for only a very short time. It is a waste of money. Think ahead, and invest in an education account, which will become a wonderful addition to a young person's future.

The Family with School Age Children

Once children start school, they need space – a room of their own away from younger siblings, for school work and for being with friends. If you have already invested in good furniture - a dresser and a chair, shelving, and a cabinet for clothes - the new room only needs a desk or a table. How a teenager's room will be decorated may not be for only the parents to decide, but you can guide and set up some rules for how much and what should be shoved into the room, unless the youngster has an after school job and can pay for things with his or her own money. In that case, you could consider selling the old furniture or using it in a younger sibling's room.

The mature couple with no children at home

When the children have left home, it is again time for big change for the parents. They will be going to 'move out' mentally, and maybe even physically. If you are 45+, you are probably living in surroundings designed for someone at least 10 years younger. Your belongings are from another period, and a step by step change should be considered. You should go through your house, and start to think about how you want to live, now that you have regained your 'freedom'. What do you want? What are the wishes and goals you want to fulfil and reach before retirement? Take into account what you think you'll be able or want to manage, both physically and financially.

You'll be wise to ask yourself a long list of questions. Have some things become more of a burden than a pleasure?

- **What do you want?**
- **What can you afford?**
- **Is the house too big now?**
- **Does it require a lot of maintenance?**
- **Is a big expense relating to the property on the horizon?**
- **Is the garden too big? – or do you love to maintain it?**
- **Have you gained other interests?**
- **Should you move into a condo?**
- **Should you keep your summer cabin?**
- **Should you move to the country/the city?**
- **Look at your current situation as well as ahead to the future. Now is the time to get rid of what only weighs you down, and make room for things and interests you really want to explore.**

And after 'Mature'...

Throughout the last few decades, older people have changed and now more and more look like the rest of the population when it comes to interests and ability to work – if they are allowed to work, that is – and divorces are not rare on the other side of 25 years of marriage. A lot of older people are travelling the world, ride motorbikes, (I was on a summer holiday trip last year to a Danish island and ran into a group of bikers with wives. Not a single person under the age of 55, and a lot of them considerably older!) and it is true: Inside an old person is a young person. Many wrinkles do not create an old mind. You are who you are all your life, and when you have reached adulthood, you don't become more ors less adventurous. The rest is decided by how lucky you are when it come to health.

So when the head is functioning well, it can be hard to accept, if the back isn't as strong as it has been, and that is why it is more important than ever to make everything a bit easier for yourself. Many old people live with furniture that is too heavy, and some get anxious about unfamiliar things. They want the same routines and the same surroundings. It is a bit strange, because the older we get, the more we can live at full throttle without a second thought. We have everything to win, and nothing to loose.

My home is a launch pad and an oasis, not a castle meant to keep out everybody and everything. For me, security is not things and walls. They can be changed or replaced. Life should be lived with people, and we must dare to do it. Otherwise we become socially poor, no matter how much stuff, or how many castles or things we possess. Security and safety can be found only inside one's head.

So should we carry around a big load of stuff we never use? A load which constantly reminds us of past times and people. Should we save everything in our lives in the form of things? No, we should not! If we do, the signal we send says that we don't live our lives, but that we have lived our lives! It is really scary, but we get stuck under the tyranny of old habits, and feel that 'new' isn't safe, so to be safe, we drag our entire past around with us!

You should make yourself realize that as an older person, you are actually part of the least vulnerable group of people, and that belongings do not provide protection. The knowledge that you can handle your everyday life does!

Many older people choose to wait to sell their house, until they are forced to by overwhelming garden work or stairs. And that is too late. The possibility of exercising choice is often taken away, and everything happens under stress and pressure, emotionally as well as timewise, all because, while they had the strength, they didn't think to imagine how they wanted to live their old age. Interestingly enough, a lot of older people regret not having made the move earlier, once they find out how easy everyday life can be, when they can again take care of themselves, without help from anybody. They don't feel helpless any more.

An old acquaintance had to move from a big house to a one bedroom apartment, because her husband had died. She was so unhappy having to move away from the place, where she had lived ever since she got married. But she had to, because she couldn't maintain the big house and garden anymore, and neither did she have the money to do so. After a short time in her lovely little apartment with a balcony in a building with an elevator, and a lot more life around her than she had in her old house, she was thriving. She didn't need any help anymore, but could handle everything herself. She said that if she had known, how nice it would be, she (and her husband) should have moved a lot sooner.

Think about how it feels not to have to ask for help all the time. To become totally independent and regain your old self, just by acknowledging your present needs. It shows that it is neither your surroundings, nor your belongings that count. It is the inner confidence and the lust for life. We don't die of living our lives, but we die, if we aren't interested in living.

So make up your mind ahead of time, where and how you would like to live in your later years. Living in a giant home, filled with stuff, needing endless cleaning and maintenance shouldn't be a goal, when you could spend your time and money living an active, independent life. You can create security by cleaning up your belongings, your finances and your living arrangements.

As a retiree, life should be filled with 'I will do...' not 'I will have to do ...'

Where are you along this timeline? Is it time for you to make some changes, or at least to give a thought to the fact that nothing stays the same!

In general: Is it time to change 'life stage'? Check to make sure you really are, where you think you are, and imagine where you will be in five years – and make a reminder to do this once a year, and/or if your life changes radically. That way changes do not seem so disturbing or even catastrophic, but will merely be something to plan for and to look forward to.

The DIY tribe are the ones, who collect anything, which they will do 'something' about at 'some point'.

The Do-You-Remember tribe are the ones, who under no circumstances can get rid of anything which has even the tiniest value as a memento.

The Waste-Not tribe are the ones, who think that giving away anything is equivalent to trashing it.

The That-is-not-polite tribe are the ones, who develop a guilty conscience over just about anything.

The Custodian tribe are the ones, who want to preserve everything for posterity.

The Guardian tribe are the ones, who ensure that nothing is lost.

The Project-Maker tribe are the ones, who start one project after another without ever finishing anything.

WIPE YOUR SLATE!

Collectors are different tribes

Collectors can be divided into different tribes:

The What-If tribe are the ones, who cannot let anything go without getting nervous about whether they may need it tomorrow.

The Cannot-Say-No-Thanks tribe are the ones, who politely receive anything offered them.

The Pleaser tribe are the ones – the tribe I belonged to – who do what is expected of them without considering if it will work for them.

These tribes have one thing in common:

They have lost control over their possessions.

There is the type whose hoarding becomes an illness. The person who cannot toss a pizzabox without feeling sick. Dealing with that takes specialists such as psychologists and a completely different approach from the one described in this book. The ones I am addressing are the ones who feel their belongings just take up too much space and energy.

WIPE YOUR SLATE!

What is hoarding?

Before going into action, we have to define the difference between hoarding and collecting.

To hoard is to receive anything you are offered, because you might be able to use it later. (in some other life!) It is when you get inspired by a thing and buy it immediately. It is when you could use anything in the whole wide world, or if you are sure you can use it later, because it seems like a good idea.

To collect is acquiring items with a common denominator. It can be anything. Donald Duck comics, furniture by a certain designer, porcelain of a special pattern or make. Collections are 'species-specific'.

But I hoarded! When I moved away from my parents, my new home was built with various leftovers from my childhood room. Great for a starter home. Later I became a single parent, and the money was not arriving in bulk, but that was OK, because there was always a nice person, who would offer a second hand sofa or chair a little bit better than the ones I already had. Something that made me very grateful, but which, I later discovered, prevented me from pulling myself together to start saving for what I really wanted. The things I got were functioning! But temporary becomes permanent, which means that you learn to manage with things, just because they are there.

When I got to the point of being able to buy the things I really wanted, I did something stupid. I stored aunt Astrid's little coffee table in the basement, because it was too good to throw out, and maybe someone would need it later. The old brass bed went the same way, because maybe some day I would need a guest bed. Or I could use it as a day bed and fill it with a lot of beautiful cushions. Right! That might happen, if ever I were to get a house big enough to have a guest room, and if the guests were no more than 5 feet tall, and, of course, if I could get a custom made mattress. Yes, then this might be possible! – please see the DIY chapter.

My time with second hand things and furniture consisted of one home, and 2 big basement rooms filled to the ceiling with more (or less) wonderful things, which I – maybe – would need later. Which I could repair, paint or re-upholster or give away if anybody was in need. There were full time jobs for a small army for 50 years in those basement rooms!

But is there anything wrong with owning many things?

YES! – If you have so many things that you push/move them around in your rooms, basements or attics, without feeling any pleasure or need for them. It is wrong, because all these things create an insurmountable 'should do' barrier in your life. Either because they should be repaired or put somewhere else, or because you can never find them, when you – or others – need them. You get negatively attached to the stuff, because you cannot find an excuse for getting rid of them. That is hoarding, and that was my problem!

Let's make it clear that hoarders are **NOT** collectors, as I will explain. The hoarders 'collect' everything – no exceptions, without being able to explain why and for no logical reason. It is extremely difficult for them getting rid of things, and for various reasons which I shall return to later.

One of my friends, whose youngest child, a daughter, had just left home, told me one day that the daughter had left an old cabinet, and "... now we will put it in the dining room, for the glasses and cups that we no longer have room for in our kitchen". A mature couple without children at home with so much kitchen equipment that they have to involve new furniture to create extra room for glasses and cups? That is hoarding! That is just more stuff not in use, because no decision was made about what to do with it.

When for some reason furniture becomes 'spare', or the household gets smaller, it is time to take a look at what your needs are now. The same idea should be applied when people buy new closets for their clothes, because they have no more space. Again, space isn't the problem. The problem is that they don't sort their clothes and don't get rid of items they don't use.

No wonder the department stores have great success with sales of plastic boxes in all sizes several times a year. They give us all a reason to put away things, we don't use 'right now', but might need some other day. Or we might even buy a new shelf, drawer, or cabinet. That is how we make it possible for the space problem to multiply! True, it is so much easier to pack stuff in a box than to make up one's mind what to do about it. But plastic boxes do not remove the 'noise and distractions' in your home. They do not improve your perspective, and they don't reduce clutter. On the contrary! (Read the chapter: A case study).

But worst of all – **our**
homes become
smaller
and smaller!

If we never remove anything, the square feet disappear little by little, as the boxes move in. Because every little plastic box we bring into the house swallows a bit of our home, which then becomes unusable. Hoarding this way is just like dining at a buffet! You eat more than you really want, and feel really bad afterwards!

To be a bit morbid about it: once you are gone, how do you think your relatives will know what was important for you, if you keep everything? How will you be remembered? Some might say that they don't care, but it matters. We picture our loved ones with what they have done and with the things that meant something to them, so if we drown this image in old junk, the picture of the person vanishes. Which legacy would you like to pass on? I want my family and my friends to know what meant something to me. They know that I see my bed, my table and chairs as utility items, and that I will change them according to my needs – my needs! – when they change. At the same time, the decorative objects I have must be meaningful and important. They are not be hidden between a lot of unimportant items. The things I value should be the only ones on display. I have a few items hidden away. They are things not suitable for sitting on a shelf. They are hidden in a small 'treasure' box in my bedroom. I will not own more treasures can be contained in that box. I am absolutely sure that I can easily remember the good times of my life without keeping an object associated with every event.

I have put a 'ceiling' on the number of my hidden treasures.

WIPE YOUR SLATE!

Mementos

A lot of us hoard memories and mementos, and they come in all sorts of shapes and disguises. It can be a place, which looks like something we once knew. It can be a sound, a smell. It can be an object, which reminds us of when we were kids, teenagers, daughters or sons, in love for the first time, newlyweds, first time parents – continue the list yourself.

We store things, which remind us of a success, a failure (it is really strange, but a lot of people save things, which refresh bad memories!), when we were happy, unhappy, too fat, too thin, too red haired... **TOO MUCH!**

We save a lot of things we don't need, and which we don't really care much about, but we keep them, because they stir something in us. Not because they have any real value.

A memento can be a special mug you used to drink from at special occasions – during summer holidays in the country, for example - or the scarf you got when you turned 17, or the small spoon your grandchild used for digging in the dirt at the summer cabin.

A sofa can also 'contain' a lot of memories. You may have had loads of good conversations on it, comforted your sick child on it, made love on it, fought, or slept ... But do you save a sofa, when it is worn out? No, you don't. You can be a bit sad, when you get rid of it, but it goes, and you look forward to the new one. That is how our relationship with most of our possessions should be. It is a healthy approach.

If you save every single little thing reminding you of your children/ grandchildren, your parents, or your boyfriend, you will very quickly get a storage problem. So discriminate. Save only the super special things. The size of things makes a difference – good and bad: It is a lot easier to save a dried flower, a porcelain figurine, and other small stuff. A lot easier than a sofa, and for exactly that reason, a lot of unimportant things are saved. It is remembrance-glue – don't waste any energy on that. An awful lot of homes are filled with valuable items (memory- or money-wise – no matter) which aren't noticed, because they disappear in the mass of too much unimportant stuff.

We owe it to ourselves to live our lives as we are now! Not as we were. Memories should not be measures in kilos or tonnes. It is not the quantity, that counts, but the quality. The important things should come out in the light. The rest is just a heavy burden that has to go.

Defining what a collection is makes it easier to distinguish between hoarding and collecting things:

A collection is not just a lots of things we find charming. It is not cute things we buy on impulse. A collection contains things fitting within the same category and with similar provenance. It is often specific things that you search for, buy and/or trade, f.ex.:

- **Stamps**
- **Tin soldiers**
- **Ballpoint pens**
- **Old toys**
- **Golf balls**
- **Theatre programs**
- **Beer bottles from different breweries – unopened!**

Collections may consist of items with the same theme. Some people collect furniture made by a certain designer or from a specific period and put together an entire home that way. Others collect things made from a particular material (bone, clay, stone etc.).

Children's collections are usually contemporary. They contain things which are collectable right now. Adults often collect something from the past.

Real collections have some definable common denominators:

Collections can become complete.

Collectors meet in clubs, on the net, where they trade, sell, and have ongoing interactions.

A collection also has its limits: It can be a baseball fan's **Red Socks** memorabilia, but never **Red Socks** memorabilia and an autograph by Bill Clinton.

Collections can become more valuable for each added item – but not necessarily monetarily.

A collection is orderly, otherwise it very quickly turns into hoarding.

A collection consists of both the things collected and the work invested in it.

Collecting is driven by interest.

A collection is established over time.

And very often you have already started collecting, long before you realize that what you have is a collection.

One of my colleagues collects Herge's Tin-Tin comics. But he has a very specific criterion for collecting them. Otherwise it would be a very small collection, as there are only a few Tin-Tin stories. On his travels, he discovered a copy which wasn't identical to the Danish version. That caught his attention, and as he travels a lot, he started searching in other countries to see, if he could find other differences in this special edition. So now he has a collection of 'Destination Moon' – in many languages. His goal is to collect all the different copies of that specific story, and he is in contact with other Tin-Tin fans around the world.

Among my friends is married couple who collects old uniforms, which you can see in their home together with the weapons and history connected to them. The weapons hang on the walls as decoration together with paintings from the same time periods, and they have two old shop mannequins dressed in original uniforms. It is a very beautiful and special home, where the collection is part of the styling.

So you can collect anything, and it is often a mystery how a collection starts – but it is never a random pile of things. There is always a common denominator.

Contemporary 'collections'.

Every year around Christmas, new collectable objects are launched. Things which appear every year as a new version of the same item. Spoons, mobiles, candlesticks etc. It is a good commercial gimmick, and it is often things which are semi expensive with an exclusive 'glow'. But the complete collection is not necessarily worth much, even if you have spent a small fortune acquiring it.

Value will always be a matter of demand, and when all of Denmark is buying these same things, the value goes down. So think about how many Christmas mobiles you really need, and buy only if you really love the thing.

There are many commercial tricks, and one of them is to launch a new object as a collector's item – from day one. This is an advertising stunt only, and don't ever let a company tell you what is a collector's item. Becoming a collector's item is a natural process, and don't let yourself be lured into collecting something just on the manufacturer's say so. Be aware of whether you fall for something because it has become a 'fad', or because you will be really happy about owning it.

So, if it is a new launch, and it is not a numbered, limited edition, don't bite. It is allowable to control your enthusiasm and instead let your healthy skepticism work.

Storing and exhibiting collections and mementos

Mementos and collections should be displayed in one place, sorted in color or size, in a glass cabinet or on shelves, so they are a daily pleasure to look at and care for. Who says that we have to have reproductions of Monet, Picasso or other paintings on our walls? I assume that not too many of us have originals painted by these two gentlemen. It can just as well be a beautiful collection, which tells something about the people living there. By exhibiting the things you love, you will show who you are. And you will be happy looking at it every day.

Assemble the collection and the mementos. Make space. Don't spread them around the house. That way you show the knowledge and care that you invested in them. It is you showing a personal side of yourself.

So when you clean up your house, don't remove the collections and important mementos. You should make space for them by eliminating the unimportant junk and clutter.

WIPE YOUR SLATE!

DIY

Do it yourself – DIY – sounds like a good idea. A healthy and fun idea. AND, it can devour enormous amounts of time and money, not to mention act as a scary stress factor.

DIY is often inspired by glossy lifestyle magazines. We see stunning homes, beautiful clothes, lovely gardens, and we read articles about people, who have rebuilt and styled these big houses and thought out the landscaping. Pulled down walls. Painted and put up wallpaper, renovated bathrooms the size of ordinary people's living rooms, new kitchens and bedrooms. We see people, who design and sew their own clothes, and people who are artistic. We read, get inspired and ambitious – we 'swallow the hook'. I can do that, too!

Hello enthusiasm – goodbye realism. How many of us haven't in a moment of totally unrealistic, creative optimism caved in?

All fired up by the good idea, we start researching where to buy the different materials, visit different stores, buy wall paper, paint, cement, knitting yarn, brushes, or whatever is needed. At any rate, a lot of equipment and tools are bought for the project. We often pay a small fortune – but it will be fun – and very personal! And then we get started.

Maybe not right now, because right now we don't have the time, but next weekend. Because all of a sudden we have realized that we are standing in front of something big. Far more time consuming and far more comprehensive than we, in our excitement, anticipated, and maybe not quite as easy as described, if we have to be honest with ourselves.

Or we find out, once we have started, that we aren't really as good as we expected at painting, hanging wall paper or mixing cement, and then it might not turn out quite as we had imagined. Half way into the project we stop, and it becomes a pile of regret and self reproach.

What is the solution?

A lot of us want to create something, and of course we don't have to buy everything, if we feel like making something personal. It can be fantastic to design clothes, decorate, paint etc.

But don't do it, unless you have the time and desire to do it. And most importantly – finish the projects. One at a time. Because if your efforts don't produce finished, useful, beautiful or fun results, they just become long walks between half done projects.

I have sewn so many curtains – simple ones with gathering tape at the top and a hem at the bottom! Voila, no big deal. So when my son wanted curtains with folds, I thought: that looks simple. But it wasn't! At least not for me. I was never satisfied. The 'fold' didn't work for me the way I wanted, and it wasn't as cheap as I had anticipated. So even though my son was a good son and reminded me that professionals would have charged a lot of money, I still got a bit annoyed with myself, when I visited him (he has moved now, and the curtains are gone!). I wanted so badly to give him those curtains, but I should have analyzed the gap between thought and end result, and I should have used professionals instead. There is a reason for people getting an education in different areas, leading to them becoming professionals. We cannot be experts at everything.

The Fleamarket fans form a vulnerable group. If you frequently attend flea markets, you find many useful 'treasures'. A small piece of furniture, you just have to fix a little, and there really are people who can make this work. But there are even more people who end up with yet another unused piece of furniture in the already crammed basement. One more thing that 'just needs a finish'.

So when you see something that 'screams' at you:" Look at me!
I have a lot of potential", there are some questions which should
ALWAYS pop up on the light banner:

- **Is it realistic to believe that I will make this?**
- **When exactly will I get the time to make this?**
- **How long will it take?**
- **How much money will it cost?**
- **Will the result be something I can be proud of?**
- **Do I really need it?**

Stop, now –

I can hear somebody yell

"home made is well made and personal".

Yes, maybe – but as mentioned before – only for some of us, and
doing it yourself often means investing a lot of money in a project.

*Back in my twenties, I decided to make a work desk myself,
because I didn't have a lot of money. My motto: How difficult
can it be? – as in 'I can do that', which is a very fine motto
in many situations. It might just be wise for me to use it
with a bit more care, because it has also put me in a lot of
strange, fun, bizarre and unwieldy situations!! And in some
quite exhausting ones.*

*But I bought a piece of plywood, table legs, sandpaper,
paint, lacquer, screws, glue, edges and carried all of it home
– on my bike! And I made it –phew! I was bored stiff by the
time I gave it the fifth layer of lacquer, and my small home
was turned upside down for quite some time in order to
make space for the workshop. But it became a desk! A desk
which looked exactly like what it was: A homemade painted,*

lacquered piece of plywood with legs! The size was perfect, and it was OK – close to nice actually - and I was quite proud of my work. But I was also annoyed at having to admit that it had cost me more than would have been the case if I had bought a desk from a furniture store. And then, I would also have had 3 drawers and a shelf for my computer. I will not even mention the time it took me to make it!

So be realistic and honest with yourself. Make things only if you have the talent and the discipline, so you don't just end up piling more stuff in the basement.

I cannot repeat it too many times: People get drained of energy by having a lot of half done projects. If you have a pile of **unfinished objects**, you will probably move them around so as to find new space for another project, and when you do, you will tell yourself: It is really too lame that I can't seem to pull myself together... some fine day I am going to... when I get the time...

It is not a good idea to invite bad feelings like this, particularly, when you are the one in control of it.

So if you are in doubt – even just a bit – about your unfinished, half dead projects, then drop them. Clean out your guilty conscience. Give them all away to somebody else, who might do something about them. But if you do, you have to realize that you might become envious when you see their finished results – but such is life. Getting rid of them will ease your mind and make room for things, that you actually want to do. You are getting stressed by the 'noise' of all the self inflicted duties, and the sum of it all drains away energy, so you will have no power to do anything at all. "I have so many projects lying around that I don't know where to start" – and then it becomes easier not to start at all. "I will do it some other day, when I have the energy. At least more energy than I have today".

Of course we shouldn't stop working with wood, quilt, sew and knit, or whatever you might be doing, but to bully ourselves with DIY-ideas is stupid. It has to be the desire turning the engine. So if you absolutely have the desire to try something you have dreamed about, without being quite sure if you have the talent, then choose a project at the easier end of the difficulty scale and finish it. Prepare yourself for trying it out. Practice makes perfect, or at least you get better, and be prepared to re-do things. But don't start one new project after another thinking that the next one will be better, because it will not! This is clearly shown in the "Case Study" chapter, in my interview with a client who went through a gigantic clean up. He expresses it very accurately.

One of the very important points about this is that you don't buy anything for a new project, until you have decided the day/week to make it. You must not pile up 'dead' stuff in your home. Nothing should lie around for months. Your projects must be 'alive'.

As you can read about throughout the book, I have a lot of experience with starting projects, and one of them was a cushion. I had bought the pattern, the yarn and the fabric to embroider a victorian cushion, and I worked on it every second or third month. The material was quite expensive, but the fact that it would take years or decades to finish it, if ever, made me give it away. I never missed it! And it had been lying around for so long that it no longer fit the changed style of my home!

So to you, who are planning a project:
Make a project plan. Calculate the time and expense, and acknowledge that many plans equate to no plans, because the priority disappears.

And to you, who have a lot of unfinished projects:
Sort your piles and find one thing you want to finish. Then give the rest away or take it to a second hand store. Plan when to make the chosen project and start making it into something useful.

Rather just one finished project, than 10 layers of guilty conscience.

WIPE YOUR SLATE!

It IS indeed difficult to clean out

There are all kinds of programs about hoarders and redesigning homes. In magazines, newspapers, and TV shows. It is good entertainment. We have had charming TV hosts running home renovations, with every place being turned into homes which, 1-2-3 voila, have become beautiful and manageable. Rooms have been cleared, new paint on the walls, small repairs (sometimes big ones) have been made, only a few pieces of basic furniture have been left, simple effects, fresh flowers and candle light complete the picture.

Magic – All the mess is gone!

It is so simple, isn't it? You just have to clean up and throw out, splash a bit of paint on the walls, and it is a done deal. Or is it? No, unfortunately not. It is not simple at all, because if it were, you would just do it. It is in fact very, very difficult, and this is one of the many reasons for me having written this book.

There are so many factors, which may put a stop to a clean-out, and the biggest one is feelings! You cannot prevent the occasional panic attack and feelings that make you want to give up, but if you try to define why you feel bad, it gets easier along the way. Not easy, but easier.

For some people the mere thought of cleaning up in their belongings is so unmanageable that they think it would be easier to move away from it all and start over again! Most of us don't have the heart just to turn our backs on the whole mess and drive away. But it could be tempting – and maybe a little bit exciting?

I have done that on a small scale. I had two basement storage rooms, as already described, and one wall was attacked by mould and had to be fixed, so I had to move all my stuff to another basement room. At that point of my life, I hadn't realized that I would have to get rid of a lot of my belongings, but there was a little voice inside me, starting to make noises. So I moved all the 'good' things – way too many – into the new basement room, contacted a charity organization and said: You can have it all, but the room has to be totally empty, when you are done. I did this without looking in the remaining boxes. I hadn't opened them in years, and had no idea what was in them!

When they arrived, I went up to my apartment, drank at least 7 cups of coffee and ate a lot of Danish pastry in order to calm my nerves. The organization was connected to a scout group, and one of the small scouts came to use my bathroom. He was dirty, with rosy cheeks and full of energy, and said: Hey Lady, you have some really good stuff! My stomach started aching, but I kept calm. When they were gone, I went down to have a look. I looked at an empty basement room with a totally bare concrete floor, and to my surprise, all I felt was relief. It was liberating. Unfortunately, something told me that it was a one time thing, and that it was not the best way to proceed, but I never regretted it, and never missed anything. Afterwards my 'collection' started growing again, because I hadn't made up my mind about what I actually needed. I ended up with the same hoarder system as before.

So accept the nervous feelings and start. It won't kill you! The 'worst' that will happen is that you will feel so much better afterwards. The result is so much worth it!

But I will admit that after I had made the final plan for my clean up, some time went by, before I took the first step. It took a lot of deep breaths. So what prevented me from just starting?

I
DID
!

When I started on this mission, I felt very insecure and nervous. I felt that I was discarding my past, as if it had been worth nothing. I felt that it became a confrontation with my past.

But I kept going, because deep inside I knew that I wouldn't find any peace until I fulfilled my plan, and after a while, I realized that I wasn't discarding anything. I was saying goodbye. Goodbye and thanks for a good time. It turned into a goodbye to the things I didn't need anymore, so I could move forward without that heavy load. I had come far supported by these things, and now I was ready to let go of my crutches and walk. I could walk without support.

The feelings which make it difficult:

Waste

We cannot get rid of anything = Use and throw away is a waste of resources. Therefore, we also don't say no to things offered to us.

Use and throw away is not ideal. But if we didn't accumulate so much, it would not be a big problem. That is a really good reason for thinking carefully, before we buy new items. Saving old things forever, because you might find a use for them at some point in the future, does not belong in this category. Things can get too old (without becoming relics) or so complicated to use compared to newer versions, that they just make life unnecessarily difficult. Keeping things indiscriminately just adds difficulty to your everyday life.

Anxiety and Insecurity

We get insecure when we give something away = Having given it away would be a shame, if maybe I will need it later – even if that doesn't happen for the next 20 years!

You have to be realistic. If years go by between the use of something, you don't really need whatever it is.

Nostalgia

If you look up the word nostalgia is says: "... dreamy longing for the past ...".
We can do a lot in our lives, but we cannot go back in time.

Nostalgia becomes negative, if it prevents us from going forward. Unfortunately, we frequently prefer to keep something familiar, even if it makes us feel bad, rather than exchanging it for something new and better. It has always been a mystery to me, why people who have experienced bad times, bad marriages and such, continue to live in the same surroundings with the same things, which connect them to bad memories, instead of starting over and shaking off the past. Even things connected to good memories are bad, if they make us stay in the past. You should never cling to 'bygone glory'. It is not healthy, but if you find yourself doing that, you should examine why you don't feel any 'glory' now. It is better to work at giving new or less stuff a chance.

Guilty Conscience

Receiving a gift or inheritance, we often equate the gift with the giver or past owner, and we feel bad, if we don't like the item, and therefore don't know what to do with it, or even if we just don't have the space or need for it.

When we think of the different reasons for not passing on gifts, we have to think about how we ourselves give gifts. I always let the receiver know that they are welcome to exchange my gift for something else, because I want my gift to make somebody happy, not to become a burden. If my gift hasn't made the receiver happy, then my money has also been wasted!

I do this because I have to admit that I sometimes buy presents on the run! Gifts that maybe aren't quite as well chosen, as I would want them to be. I always buy with the best of intentions, but sometimes I am not so lucky/good at finding the right object. Well, that's me, and I am quite sure that it is you too, sometimes. I have at times been at the point of not having a clue what to buy, and then I have grabbed the first thing I thought would be good and bought it. So all presents are not necessarily bought with deep feelings, even when our feelings for the receiver are deep and warm.

Regardless of how we look at it, the fact is that a gift belongs to the receiver and not to the giver, and the receiver can do with it exactly as he/she likes. Of course, we shouldn't hurt each other, but should accept that neither the gifts we give, nor the ones we receive, can always be absolutely perfect. So we shouldn't expect of each other that all gifts be kept forever.

So how to get rid of an unwanted gift? Preferably exchange it in the shop where it was bought for something you need, or, if that is not possible, for a gift certificate for the amount, which gives you time to think about what you need. If an exchange is not possible, you can give it away to a charity organization or a second hand store which supports a charity you like, or you can try to sell it.

Heirlooms

The first thing to remember is that you are not the custodian in a museum for your ancestors, and that it is wrong to imbue items with a soul. Heirlooms have never belonged to you. They are things left to you, and unless you have made a deal with the person who passed on, you are not obliged to keep these things. If you want, choose a couple of things that can find a natural place in your home, and let go of the rest.

For me, photos are important mementos, which show how my family looked through generations, how they lived, and show situations from their everyday life. So when I had to clear my family home, after my father passed on, I chose the old albums, which, for me, compose the family treasure and history. They had their place in a small chest, which I also took, together with a small tobacco wall cabinet. I made space in my home for both pieces. The tobacco cabinet became my CD-cabinet, and I gave away my CD-holders. The small chest has become the storage place for my sewing machine.

When I asked my son what he wanted from his grandparents, he decided on an old transistor radio from the '50s, which accompanied his Grandfather around the house, and an old wall clock which dates back to his great-great-grandparents. What was left was given away, and I felt good about that.

Especially in a situation like this you have to limit yourself, even though it is very difficult. Choose only a few things. You must choose not to live in a museum for deceased family members.

Another thing to remember is that you should not choose something, just because you think it had value for the deceased person, because it will most often just be an assumption. The painting that hung over the sofa 'for ages' may have been there for no particular reason, not necessarily because it was a favourite painting. Just because something was on display, does not mean it was a favourite thing. Maybe it was a gift from a mother-in-law! So choose things you really like and connect with the person, so it becomes a pleasure to have them and the history that goes with them. Try to look around your own home to see, if you have any 'habit' things. You probably do.

Purchasing Mistakes

In a clean up you will often experience that it can be difficult to deal with things having financial value. You might have bought something, that turned out to be a mistake, and the feeling that you have wasted your money, can make it very difficult to accept having to get rid of it. It feels like a failure. It is a mistake, and gives you a bitter taste. You find it hard to admit and then you cannot persuade yourself to let it go, because it is money out the window. But this is actually one of the most important feelings to recognize when you clean out: Learn to say a nice goodbye and let go. In the above described situation you should say goodbye, so you don't continue your mental self flagellation.

We all buy things, which turn out to be mistakes. And yes, it is so annoying, but why have a pair of shoes in a shoe box taking up space in your closet, when you have worn them only once or twice, and you know for sure that they make your feet boiling hot, give you blisters, hurt your big toe, are too heavy, or should have been a size bigger, or whatever the mistake is. Or you bought a jacket or a dress, which (you reluctantly have to admit) didn't quite fit, but was nice and quite cheap, and when you have lost those 5 pounds, it will be perfect! Or the giant kitchen appliance supposed to revolutionize your cooking talents.

As pointed out, we all make mistakes, and I will share one of mine, which still makes my friends laugh out loud! I visited a good friend, who had the most beautiful little rococo chair, so comfortable to sit on. It really needed re-upholstering, but you could easily see how beautiful it would be with the right fabric. The owner was willing to sell the chair, but in her basement (!!!) she also had another chair and a two-seater in the same style. A whole set. You already see the picture, don't you? It was in the basement – and I should have left it there, but it was cheap! I was totally fired up! I could have a whole new living room at a very low cost, and my sofa looked exactly like what it was: A 10-year old Ikea sofa, which had had a very good life with a lot of living. But I imagined this stylish rococo set in my living room, bought it and brought it home. And then the 'party' started. I contacted an upholstering company, which came and gave me an estimate for bringing the furniture up to date. They brought fabric samples, and I fell for one in particular – of course, a fabric from the most expensive fabric binder. It cost me a fortune to have the set upholstered, and don't ask, where I had put my brain. BUT the result was very, very beautiful. In fact, far more so than I had hoped for.

At that point, I lived in an apartment with a long narrow living room which functioned best by being divided into two sections. So the whole rococo set was placed by the window. It was wonderful. Family, friends and others came to see it, and all agreed. They all said: Wonderful, fantastic! – and then they sat down on the Ikea sofa. So did I. I must admit that it took some time for me to finish the thought: I have made a huge mistake! I have never before (nor after) made a mistake of those dimensions. It was beautiful, but it didn't invite you to curl up in a corner and have a cup of tea and read a book. It was a set of furniture which demanded you sit up straight and be formal. It felt good for your back sitting there, but it wasn't cosy.

I didn't know what to do, and the feeling was killing me, so I called a person, who had knowledge about old furniture and told my story. She listened very nicely and patiently to my long speech, and then she said: "Sell the crap!" and added: "Get rid of it and move on. There is no reason to whip yourself with things, you do wrong. Just learn from it, and don't ever do it again!". So I contacted an auction house, and sold the whole lot – at a big loss. But it was a beautiful rococo-set!

I became quite a lot poorer and a whole lot wiser, and today I look back at it and I can share the laughs.

There are so many beautiful things in the world, but I don't need to own them all, and not every beautiful thing is right for me. Now there are things I just enjoy looking at– in the shops, the magazines and at friends's houses - and that costs nothing.

So sort through your belongings and find the things you have invested in, which aren't really 'you'. The things you never use. The things nicely stored in boxes or on hangers – untouched.

Fill a big plastic bag with those things, take it to your local second hand store and leave it there! Don't waste time trying to get a few bucks out of them. Just leave! Somebody, who needs them will be happy.

And when you go through the store, close your eyes to all the stuff, which might tempt you! From now on you don't bring anything over your threshold, without being totally sure about having a use for it. Second hand stores sometimes do have little treasures, but more not than often. Buy a cookie instead!

Result Anxiety

Result anxiety can be a very big hurdle. The feeling that you will not succeed, and that you don't know where to start can stop many a good intention to clean out, and you may find a lot of 'good' excuses not to start, such as "It will not work anyway", or

I would really like to start, but I am having guests next Friday, and then it is the weekend;

I don't know where to put the things from the big closet;

I don't have the money for modern-
izing afterwards, once I get all that
space;

I don't have the time;

Even though I hate it, I really cannot
give away that bowl. It belonged to
uncle Alfred;

Maybe I will miss it some day, and
then I will regret having tossed it;

When I get the time, I will make
'something' out of it;

What is your excuse?

This is all insecurity. Ignore it and continue. There can be many
blocking feelings, but your fantasy will always outdo reality. Once
you start, it will work. It is – only – a question about getting started.

There could be other obstacles, and they might be well inten-
tioned: The family!
Maybe you are the only one in your home feeling the need to
clean up and clean out, and it can be difficult to motivate other
family members. There will often be one member of a family, who
has no problems living with piles and boxes, so if you meet big
resistance, you have to acknowledge that you can only deal with
your personal stuff. But this is not entirely negative. Eventually, it
will rub off on the surroundings, and then you can quietly come
to the 'rescue'.

So, as you are doing your thing with a gentle hand and respecting other family members' belongings, you should let go of feeling responsible for things that aren't yours. You have to leave the family to take care of their own stuff. And just as you respect their ways and accept that they don't want what you want, you must demand that they respect and accept your new rules for your belongings. Mind your own business and let others do what they want. Just wait and see. When something is functioning, others will follow suit.

Prepare everybody for what you are going to do, but don't roll it out with the big guns. Nobody must feel that you are a one man army on a punitive expedition or a missionary among pagans. Make your plan visible without going into details. Start quietly and calmly. Sort your own things. Put boxes and plastic bags where everybody can see them, and make it clear that they are your things, and nothing – absolutely nothing – in them may be removed once put there. – That rule goes for yourself too.

There will always be fear when getting rid of something 10, 20 or 30 years old. But old is not the same as valuable, either monetarily or when it concerns feelings. It is only familiarity holding you back, and insecurity and a guilty conscience will be two very difficult companions during the whole process, but they get weaker along the way, and the more confidence you gain moving forward with the plan, the freer you will feel. But crises may occur:

Halfway through my clean-up I hit a crisis in the form of a big bag of fabrics. I have always been crazy about fabrics. By the yard! There were loads of fabrics that I had bought, whenever I passed fabric stores. Particularly if there was one of those boxes with remnants. I could always find something that would make a smart jacket, or a nice skirt, aprons for girlfriends, lunch napkins in the right colours, and... and...

and...

When I found the box again, all these plans reappeared in my head, while I looked through the bag – right until I looked at a piece of fabric for the 117th time. I had bought it to make kitchen curtains for the new apartment, I was going to buy and ended up not buying anyway! The fabric was 12 years old! But it was still quite cute, and I could actually make a quilted bed spread from it! The plans for what I could do with it came at lightning speed, but in my inner core a feeling of guilty conscience started growing – guilty conscience by the yard. So I stopped my brain spin! When, for 12 years, I hadn't taken the opportunity to make anything with it, my common sense told me that I never would. I put it back in the plastic bag, went to a girlfriend who sews all the time, said: "for you", put down the bag, and left. My friend thought it was funny, and that she had been given a gift. When I got home, I was euphoric! I had once again removed a self-inflicted feeling of guilty conscience! I could stop beating up myself about one more thing that I would never get done.

So be prepared **– situations will arise in which you feel like being stuck in glue up to your neck**, but they are feelings connected to old habits, nothing that will hurt you. Your inner security blanket has to be convinced that feeling secure and having things aren't the same.

SO BELIEVE IN IT!

When you start at big project, you often think it through from A to Z, and you get so overwhelmed that you give up before you start, because the task is too big. You get future-paralyzed. You are looking to the end, instead of looking to the next point – to the next stepping stone. The all encompassing view can be paralyzing.

Some clever and witty person (A lovely variation on Creighton W. Abrams, Jr.) once came up with this gem: How do you eat an elephant? Answer: One bite at a time!

WIPE YOUR SLATE!

Advice for styling the rooms in your home

Before you start on your mission, it is a good idea to make a plan for how you want your home to end up looking. Think of how your expectations will lead to the result. As I have mentioned earlier, I am not an interior decorator, but I have quite a lot of experience with what works. Make a plan for one room at a time.

The Living Room

For each room, begin by moving everything into another space – if possible. The living room should be organized so the family can relax, be together, and have meals together, unless that happens in a kitchen dining area or separate dining room. The whole family has to be able to watch TV, and you should plan for storage space. If the family plays a lot of games and has toys there, space should be made for them, and it is a good idea to have a piece of furniture, where you can easily put away everything that is not in use. Shelves for books and magazines are necessary, so a cabinet with doors is a good investment. Rather one big cabinet than two small ones, because too many small pieces of furniture make for a messy look.

Here is one indisputable fact:

You never NEED knick knacks.

The decorative objects entering your home should be chosen with great care. They shouldn't be there for no good reason, because they do become dust collectors. So put all of them in a box and put that away for 2 weeks. If by then, you really miss some of them, then put them back – but only the ones you cannot live without – and let the leftovers go to a charity or sell them.

Books take up a lot of space and look nice. If you read a lot, I am sure that you have many books you will never read again. Pass them on to family and friends with the message to do the same when they have read them. Books that are just collecting dust on a shelf are of no value to anybody. So keep the books which really mean something to you, and let the others go.

A TV is a demanding piece of furniture. It takes up space, attention, and time, and will never win a design prize, no matter the brand. It is difficult to ignore a turned on TV, regardless of your interest, or lack thereof, in what is being shown. You can save a lot of space and time by not having one in each room. Personally, I don't think a TV belongs in bedrooms or children's rooms. It disturbs sleep and relaxation, and should not be used as a babysitter. Having a TV turned on during dinner is a bad idea. That should be the time of the day, when the whole family gets together and talks about what has happened in everyone's lives.

"Every day without TV is a good day"

quote by my son, who thinks that if he didn't have time to sit in front of the TV, his time has been spent doing something better.

The Bedroom

Again, move everything out. The exception would be the bed and closets, if you have any there. Dressers and extra pieces of furniture should be placed elsewhere for the moment, and you have to empty everything. Everything! Place it on the floor or in a room close by. Under bed storage units too. Those plastic or wooden boxes that you can roll under the bed. They have to go. They play havock with both easy cleaning and air circulation. Dust balls are not good to have in a room where you sleep. They are not desirable anywhere, but here especially, it is important that the air is fresh and clean. Start cleaning the room and move back the furniture you cannot do without. But discriminate. Do you need the small table that used to be there? Did it have a function? If not, it does not go back.

Don't worry about the fact that you now have 2 closets and 2 dressers and piles of everything on the floor. You will take care of that, when you toss the stuff you don't use. I promise that if you clean up this way, the pile you keep will be only a third the size of the pile you cannot use. You will need a lot less storage space.

Closets and Clothes

The way we dress sends signals to the world about how we want to be perceived, and that is definitely important. But is it really something we should take so seriously that we cannot get rid of a garment when it is worn out, or doesn't fit anymore? If you look at it objectively, they are pieces of fabric or knit, with which we cover our bodies for the purpose of not freezing or sweating. There isn't anything more to it, and there are no reasons to connect your feelings to your clothes. They come and go.

For clothes there are 3 rules:

Are they ruined?

If they are torn or have spots, that cannot be removed, they have to go. If you at some point in time couldn't mend them, or if you haven't even made the effort to try, don't kid yourself, you will not do it now. Out they go!

Do they fit?

I only have to loose 10 pounds, then it will fit! Forget it! If you first have to lose weight, you can be sure that your butt will not have the same shape as before you became 'rounder'. The size might fit, but the shape probably won't. So put it in a plastic bag, and take it to a charity.

Have I used it during the last 12 months?

If you haven't used it this season or the previous one, there is probably a reason! Maybe it doesn't quite fit, it crinkles, it scratches, or the colour doesn't match anything else in your closet. Also, things like table cloths needing a lot of ironing after being washed, linen requiring the same, and towels which after 5 times in the laundry still won't dry you – everything goes!

When you have gone through it all – **all of your clothes**, linen, towels, and don't forget your underwear, you have **3** piles:

One for the **garbage**;

One for the **second hand store**;

And one pile of what you can **actually** use - a **shockingly small one**.

Now the **PANIC** sets in! **HELP!** NOW I HAVE NO CLOTHES LEFT!

Yes, you have. You have just as many clothes as before. You have only removed the stuff you didn't use anyway!

Better a closet with a few good things, which fit you, than a closet sending a signal about you having become fatter, skinnier, or older. So get rid of the tops reminding you of being 17 and able to go braless! You are the person you are right now, and you deserve to look good. That is only possible in clothes which fit your body, your age and the life, you live.

To look into a closet, that all of a sudden echoes, is a new and wonderful experience:

You can see, what you have
You can see, what you are missing
- and you can see when you need to do laundry!

One of the 'side effects' is that you can now write a wish list of what you need to optimize your wardrobe: a white shirt, a pair of brown boots etc. It becomes easy not to be tempted by things, which do not fit in.

I am not a fan of colour tyranny. The dictate, for example, that you have to wear autumn colours, if you have red hair and green eyes. I think you should do what makes you feel good. But it makes good sense to stick to some basic colours which match. It helps you avoid purchasing things you will never use. You can always buy cheaper, and for the time being fashionable, items that can be thrown out, when you get tired of them. But the basic wardrobe should be limited to a maximum of 3 neutral colours.

One argument I hear often is: "But everything has its revival", take vintage clothes for example, so maybe it is a good idea to keep your clothes any way? There are only few of us who can get away with wearing second hand clothes. Some people do, and I am quite sure that takes a special talent. But the root of that talent is that you are 17 years old, and look amazing no matter what you wear, and therefore get away with it. Second hand clothes most often look like exactly what they are: second hand clothes!

There are two kinds of clothes: Seasonal clothes and all year clothes. So go through your clothes at the start of every season. At the end of a season, when you put them away, you cannot look at them objectively, after having just worn them for months. It has often surprised me, when I unpack them again, how dull and worn the clothes looked, that I wore the previous season. Go through the all year clothes at the same time. It is often an eye opener, and something you otherwise never get to do, because you just leave them hanging there year after year. This way you will have no 'dead' clothes in your closet making it look as if you have loads of clothes and shoes, while still feeling that you never have a thing to wear.

'Dead Clothes'

I once had to attend a big party and needed something new to wear, so I went to a department store to find a top. I ended up looking at some French blouses. A very sweet sales woman came and asked if she could help me. We discussed the blouses that I fancied, and she immediately pull one out and said: "This one! The others are so unique that you can use them only a few times, and then you will have spent a lot of money on a piece of 'dead clothing' hanging in your closet." That expression has followed me ever since. I strive NOT to have any dead clothes in my wardrobe. I had that blouse for 8 years, and I have now given it away.

Back to the clean-out.

Now you put your small pile of clothes and accessories back in your closet and dresser. I am sure you have room for it all now - if you have been faithful about sorting things in accordance with the 3 rules.

Linen

You go through the same procedure with your bed linen, duvets, blankets, pillows etc. Ask yourself how many sets of bed linen you need. I suggest choosing the best 3-4 sets for each family member: One on the bed, one in the laundry basket, one in the closet and one in reserve. Find your own system that will work with your laundry routine and family structure. Families with small people need a bit more in reserve than the family with half- and full grown family members. It is all about the number of people and their ages. But 10 sets of linen for each person are not necessary. Be tough about it. If you have relatives staying over night, you can ask them to bring their own linen, and, if convenient, their own blankets and pillows. You bring you own stuff if you spend summer holiday in a rented cottage, so you can do it, when you visit relatives. Making your home fit you and your family should always be your top priority.

The Kitchen

Kitchens are easy. Or easier. Here, it is a question of whether you use the appliances and utensils, and less about having a personal relationship with them. Of course, you may have things you like, but the kitchen is – when you get right down to it – a work space. Anything that is 'kind of' broken should go, as should everything unused for years on end. Mismatched sets add to clutter and only take up space, no matter how pretty they are. So clear all cabinets, and only put back what the family is using.

There may also be seasonal objects in a kitchen, but if you actually never use them, then give them away together with all the shiny appliances you so enthusiastically bought so you could make those new, exiting dishes that just never materialized.

Let it be a goal that you don't have to move 5 things to get to what you need to use right now. Excepting plates, don't stack things, if you can avoid it. You should not have to move 10 things to get to the right bowl, and nobody needs 6 mixing bowls.

So what do you need in a kitchen?
A well known Danish master chef, Erwin Lauterbach, once made a list of things you need in a kitchen. His view is that no new kitchen wares are invented anymore. They are all old things in new, smart wrapping, sold at quadruple the price of the old version, which still works just fine.

Here is his list – probably quite an eye opener:

- A salt bowl . . . . . . *which is easy to get to*
- A pepper mill . . . . . *big, with a good grip*
- Scales
- A measuring cup
- Ladles, scraper, spatula
- A whisk . . . . *with a few wire loops for stirring*
- A whisk . . . . *with many wire loops for whipping*
- A deep frying spoon . *to replace a skimmer that lets food slide off*
- A sieve
- A colander
- A garlic press
- A potato masher
- A potato peeler
- Tongs . . . . *for turning meat etc.*
- A big knife . . . . . . *serrated, for cutting meat, vegetables and bread*
- A herb knife
- A filleting knife
- A sharpening steel
- A casserole . . . . . . *take into account the size of your family, when choosing sizes of pans*
- A small pot
- A bigger pot
- A sauté pan . . . . . . *with a glass lid, so you can see, what is going on without having to lift the lid*
- A baking pan . . . . . *so you don't have to use the big oven pan every time*
- A frying pan
- 3 bowls . . . . *different sizes*
- 1 steel bowl . . . . . *to rapidly cool off food (it cools too slowly in a plastic bowl)*
- 3 cutting boards . . . *one for meat, one for vegetables, and one for making sandwiches*

**All together 30 pieces of kitchen ware,
that cover everything – big and small!**

So if this is what a professional chef thinks should be in a kitchen, maybe we should stop filling our cabinets with all sorts of fancy inventions, never used, just taking up space – and difficult to keep clean.

The Children's Room

Children's rooms should be simple. A chair big enough for an adult and a child to sit and read, a dresser, a small table for the toddler to draw or play at, and a small bookshelf. And a lot of space on the floor. Depending on the age of the child, there should be storage furniture, which could be boxes for the small kids, shelves for the bigger ones, and a desk for the school aged children. You could start collecting these things, when baby arrives. It should be easy to clean and the room should be airy, and ready for play.

The Bathroom

The bathroom is usually not that big, and cleaning it out not that diffcult. Again, you start by removing everything. Cabinets and shelves should be completely empty. Because of the damp environment and heat, you should never store any kind of medication in a bathroom and child proof any medicine cabinet with a lock. While sorting your medications, and do it regularly, check the expiry date. Take expired medication to a pharmacy to be disposed of properly.

ANY KIND OF OPENED COSMETICS CONTAINER IS A LIVING BACTERIA BOMB

Go through all your cosmetics. If they have an expiry date, check it. No opened tube or container should be kept for more than 4 months. Sunscreen from last year also has to go. You cannot be sure that the screening factor is still effective. Never stick your fingers in a cream. Get a spatula. It should be available in a cosmetic store or department. Don't save creams or perfumes for 'special' occasions. They have a limited shelf life. Throw out anything you haven't used for the last 3 months.

Now to the bathroom accessories. The toothbrush cups may need to be replaced – as may the soap dish, if you have one.

Now I get to one of my pet peeves: Who on earth invented the closed toilet brush holder! I would like to get my hands on that genius. It looks great, but it is so unhygienic! Imagine what lives down there in the moisture and darkness? Monsters come from there. The very best toilet brush is the humble plastic brush in an open cup. It cleans just as well as the fancy one, and it dries fast. And it has one more advantage: It is cheap, so you can throw it out with a good conscience, when it gets ugly – not that I will claim that it ever looked good. The closed in fancy designer one, which has collected nasty bacteria older than your children, is not a good idea, regardless of its good looks.

If you have cabinets in the bathroom, keep your towels, soap and toilet paper there. Make room for things, where they are being used whenever possible.

Loose items in bathrooms should be kept to a minimum. A hanging cabinet big enough for all the necessary things is always a good investment, considering the ease of cleaning and the hygiene. Store all the small items in boxes out of sight.

The Entrance

The entrance gives people their first impression of your home, and can be a difficult room to deal with, as it is often small and/ or narrow. If it is the size of a shoe box, you have to consider how many coat hooks you should have there. Hooks are fine if there is one for each coat or jacket, but quite often coats upon coats hang on one hook, taking up all the space in the room. A nearby closet might be a better solution. You need a mat for wet shoes, and a place for gloves, keys and the like. If you have enough room, a place where you can sit to put on shoes is nice. If you have the possibility of putting away things in the same place right when you get home, it becomes a habit, and a lot of time is saved by not having to look for them all over the house.

Basements and Attics

Basements and attics are often areas of total chaos, with lots of functional things that never see daylight, and often get destroyed by being pushed around, when somebody tries to find something. This is where we put things, when we haven't made up our minds about what to do with them.

I had two basement rooms, and believe me, that is one too many! They were so crammed that it was like participating in a triathlon, when I had to go there to find things, which I knew - or rather thought - I had somewhere. These basement rooms was a universe containing things I didn't need anymore, but hadn't made up my mind to get rid of. So I decided that my basement rooms should be as easy to live with as the rooms in my apartment. They should only contain things like tools, my bike, Christmas and Easter ornaments and decorations, and, during winter, the items from my balcony.

A part of this clean out became particularly difficult. When I started this quest to unload my collection of guilty conscience and ballast from the past, it rubbed off on my son. He had taken all his childhood toys with him, when he moved away from home. When he was a child, he was really careful with his toys, everything was in mint condition, and there was a LOT of it.

They were placed in his tiny basement room, and had spilled over into mine – at that time I had two such rooms. A lot of music equipment in original boxes, computer equipment, paint and wall paper leftovers etc. His basement looked like most basements do. So he asked, if I would help him, and of course I would, so we started.

My son found that he had memories connected to every single item, and couldn't make up his mind at all about what to keep, and what to get rid of. Even though he had completely forgotten about the stuff, until he held it in his hand, and even though they were things, he would never consider passing on to his future children. It was a real difficult situation, and we gave up for the time being. We both knew that we had to address the problem some other way. I suggested that he sit down and consider what he really cared about when he was a kid. I made him this questionnaire:

*Will I pass this on to my future children. Do I really want
to give this to my child, when it has been lying around in a
basement for decades?*
   Are there collections worth keeping?
   Which things do I think about first?
   - and he decided to keep these 5 things:

A big box of Lego
*A box of Brio (wooden toys), Märklin trains, radio controlled
cars,*
   and his comic books (he is still a great Marvel fan).

*Those were very strict rules, but they made it easier for
both of us, because his memories were also mine. We were
reminded of his childhood again, and the memories are still
there, but he doesn't need stacks of boxes to remember the
good times. A couple of months afterwards he said to me:
You have no idea how glad I am about the work we did in
my basement. It is so good to know what is down there, and
that it is stored properly. It is only good stuff, that my children
can play with in the future, and some mementos for myself.*

When you do a job like this, and the panic sets in, you need a
partner who isn't emotionally involved. So choose your helper
with care. Don't do as we did. Choose somebody who isn't
that close or doesn't know you too well, so you can keep it as a
minimizing project, and not a walk down memory lane.

A basement or an attic should, like any other room, not contain
'dead' stuff. They should not become junk rooms, but rather
containers for things used regularly:

Summer equipment, which has to be stored during winter and vice versa

Tools – ready for use. Nothing rusty or broken

Christmas, Easter and other similar decorations

Bikes

Garden tools, flower pots etc.

Anything having waited for repair for ages or been hidden for 'difficult' times has to go.

A Treasure Box

A treasure box is a necessity, even though it almost always contains unimportant things – when looked at objectively. It is the completely private storage space for mementos of different kinds, which, for one reason or another, we cannot have on display. Letters, a few things from childhood. Each individual will have his or her own good reasons for keeping them, but you should keep it at one box per person and an extra one for family history. You should invest in good plastic boxes with lids and wheels, and you should be able to stack them. Transparent boxes are the best. You can quickly see what is in them.

Be
Realistic

- When you clean out, don't plan design styles fitting mansions or castles, if you live in a shoe box

- It is not yet time to think details, decoration and small stuff. Concentrate on the big picture

- Use the furniture you have now and that you will keep. But remember as few pieces as possible

- Style each area of your home for the intended purpose, and don't make all rooms multifunctional. That only creates confusion, and doesn't help

- Place things 'naturally,' so they are where they will be needed

- Make room for a storage cabinet in every room whenever possible, so you have your bed linen in the bedroom, toilet paper in the bathroom, etc.

As mentioned before – many small boxes, dressers, and other kinds of furniture create a messy look. Think Big! It might seem illogical, but an entire wall with one cabinet gives more open space than several small ones spread around. This is also true for small rooms – in fact especially for small rooms!

OK!

That was it! Does this seem as if it will change anything in your life? Maybe not. But believe me, it will! When you have dealt with the whole house, you will see both how much closer you have come to have the home, you really want, and how you already have a lot of the things you need. You will feel lighter. To know exactly what you have removes a lot of 'noise' in your head, and also makes it clear whether you need something else. You can start saving for the right things. Write a wish list!

Get professional help if you feel the task is too big to handle on your own, or if you have tried time and time again without success. But remember, you need a plan setting out, what you want your end result to be. Otherwise, the project drowns in a lot of inner arguments, and you will be left with the 27 boxes you will never again open that contain things from which a lot of other people could benefit, or things you could sell to finance the purchase of something you actually need.

Friends can be of help, but are not always the best choice for support. If you stick to your plan, and have a 'weak' moment in the middle of the whole thing, it is the friend's job – according to a pre-made agreement – to challenge you. But you should be careful not to abuse your friendships, and that may be the result of this kind of arrangement. You avoid this by working with a professional.

ROOMS WITH CLUTTER CREATE NOISE
- even if you don't notice it on an everyday basis.

Even with things out of sight, they are not necessarily out of mind.

WIPE YOUR SLATE!

The Three Methods

Of course there are plenty of ways to clean out your belongings, but I will suggest the following three. The gentle, the medium, and the tough:

The Gentle One

The Gentle Method develops gradually over time, so even the very anxious declutterer can handle it, because it is the one creating the least drama. I am not really in favour of it, because it is the one most likely to fail, but I will describe it anyway. The danger is that it all 'fizzles out', because you loose the sense of how it should all end. In other words: You may too easily lose your perspective of the project in its entirety.

But – you make a plan for each room, break it into smaller sections, and mark dates in your calendar for attacking each section. If you have a bedroom with a closet, a work space, and a dresser, each piece of furniture becomes a section, and you work with these sections one at a time. It is important to finish each section, but it can – and here is one of the dangers – be difficult to see where to put things that will stay, because there is no space for them, until the other sections have also been completed. So, before starting out, you really have to think through how to do this.

The Medium One

Here you concentrate on one whole room at a time. The advantage over the Gentle Method being that you can clear a whole room, and maybe even decide to paint or make repairs, before you put things back in place. You are more likely to succeed this way, but again – finish the task. It is very important. Finish, before you start somewhere else. And mark your calendar.

The Tough One

Here you decide to go through every room in your house over a long weekend, or during holidays. It sounds tough, but you will not get the chance to stray from the plan you made before you started. Do what my client in the chapter A Case Study stuck to when he took on his big project. It becomes so much more obvious what is necessary.

No matter which method you use, it is important to empty everything. Don't start picking things from a drawer. You will get nowhere that way. All drawers, dressers, cabinets, closets and other storage spaces must be **COMPLETELY** emptied, and then you sort **EVERYTHING**. You also have to decide if you need all the furniture in the room, or if you could remove work space from the bedroom, for example – always a bad place for it, by the way. It disturbs a good night's sleep, because you can look at it when you lie down and get reminded about work, finances or whatever else, you are working on.

But even if the decision was to only handle one drawer at a time, it must be completely emptied. Always begin with empty space.

WIPE YOUR SLATE!

On your marks, get set...

We may all have heard the saying: "If you own more than seven things, the things own you". That is all very well, if you are a buddhist monk, but I don't think too many buddhist monks need to read this book.

Let us try a thought experiment: If a fire broke out – may all higher forces forbid it! – and, after all living creatures were saved, you could choose to save only 7 things, what would they be?

Your photo albums?

Your golf clubs?

Your jewels?

Aunt Anna's old vase?

Little Frederik's clay ashtray?

Your Chanel/H&M jacket?

Your old teddy bear?

The Family Bible?

Your toy train?

Your motor bike?

Or ....?

The experiment will give you a very good indication of what really means something to you. You will find out what you don't want to be without. These are the things that deserve to be dug out from between all the unimportant stuff.

This little task is an eye opener for many people. Write it down, but don't sit and chew on your pencil, just write what comes to mind. Your subconscious will yell out loud. And if it doesn't, there is an even better reason to be really tough about getting rid of things, because in that case you have been saving things of no value at all.

So write down the list of the 7 things you would be heartbroken to lose, and keep it with you as you work your way through the project. Look at the list now and then when too much ends up in the 'keep it' pile.

WIPE YOUR SLATE!

Go!

Now! Now we are almost there! You are at the starting line. What do you need to get going?

- You have to figure out how you will dispose of your things
- It could be: To friends, to a charity, sell it, to a recycling container, or all of those
- Set the date, and stick to it. If the sky falls down, and the earth cracks, stick to it. Don't let anything get in the way, once the date is set
- Buy big plastic bags.
- Buy one plastic box for each family member (for the treasures) + 1 extra for family history items
- Now you can start – and be enthusiastic about it. A good mood will carry you far.

Hundreds of good books have been written about how to do this, and if you put them in a big melting pot, the result will be like this:

1. Keep what you use, and the things you love. Emphazise USE and LOVE

2. If you haven't used an item during the past year – new or old, of value or not for whatever reason – it goes. You don't need it!

Said in another way:

1. Use/cannot live without – keep it

2. Unused for a season – OUT!

Now you keep repeating:

Point no. 1 and 2
Point no. 1 and 2
Point no. 1 and 2

Continue in this manner while sorting through EVERYTHING you own.

And one more point – if you are in doubt, it goes! Doubt is a sign that your brain and your intuition are fighting. Let your intuition win. Because you should never be in doubt about what is really important for you.

Put the stuff going to 'new homes' in plastic bags (man's best friend!), close them and put them away. Do it neatly. Put labels on the bags, so you can immediately see, what goes to charity, what is going to be sold, and what goes straight to the garbage. You can write with red, green or black. Make it visible.

If you have decided

Giving away to family and friends:

If you want to give away to family and friends, then inform them about the date, and that they have to stay away, until you call them. Once you are done, the message will be that it is now or never, because by the end of the day, you will call for pickup by a charity organization, and/or a professional buyer, and leftovers will go to recycling immediately. They HAVE to come that day, when it suits you, because YOU are the one, who have a job to finish. If they cannot, too bad! You should have absolutely nothing lying around, when the clean out is done.

On pickup by a salvage dealer:

These people sometimes demand money to remove your things. Their costs for pick up and storage have to be covered. They don't pick up anything, which will not give them a profit, and they can see what is worth something, and what isn't. So it might be better in the long run to simply pay them, just to get rid of everything.

To sell:

If you choose to sell some of your things yourself – things you know have value – you should take photos and send them to an auction house for valuations. Remember to ask what market value might be, which isn't necessarily the amount resulting from an insurance valuation. So don't get disappointed. If the things you consider valuable are not trendy right now, or if lots of people are selling the same things at the same time, you might not get quite what you expected.

Some things may be trendy now, and worthless in a year. Expensive complete collections of whatever it may be are not necessarily all that valuable if everyone else has them too. Contact a collector forum on the Internet and ask for advice before trying to sell collections.

When you have sold what you want to get rid of, reward yourself with buying something you need, and be happy. Forget about what is gone.

Giving to charity:

Contact charity organizations to find out, if they will pick up, or if you have to bring the stuff to them. These organizations are normally run by volunteers, and they work hard. There could be local scouts, youth- or sports clubs operating flea markets as fund raisers, and if giving your things to them, you will know who benefits.

On recycling:

Find out operating hours and addresses for your local recycling places. It is important to get everything out of the house as fast as possible.

Selling at a flea market:

Here are some comments about selling at flea markets and garage sales. They can be very challenging for a newly created declutterer! Actually, I don't recommend them at all. But if you have the courage to take a second look and sell your things that way, be aware that it is not that easy. It becomes difficult, when a buyer is standing in front of you saying: "Look at that beautiful candle stick. It would look fantastic on my night stand". The danger is that we often see a new value in things, when somebody else wants them, and it is not good, if that makes the item come 'back home'.

Just like when a relationship ends, you often feel a false longing, when somebody looks affectionately at your ex-partner, because all of a sudden you can see what originally charmed you. But you know deep inside that it won't work. It is exactly the same when it comes to things.

And then one may hear about people, who have sold stuff at flea markets for huge amounts of money. That may be a truth with a twist. You never hear how big a job it is packing the stuff, getting up at dawn, the weight of all the boxes, the long drive, the unpacking, the standing freezing or sweating for hours, and the whole thing in reverse – with sales for maybe 30 bucks at the end of the day. You have to think it is fun selling at a flea market. Otherwise, drop the idea and get someone to come and pick up the whole load. Out of sight is out of mind.

Anyone who has been at a flea market knows that prices can be haggled down to virtually nothing. And that is exactly what happens, when you are on the other side of the table: You find that nobody is prepared to buy for the price you think is reasonable, no matter how valuable the item is. For example: hand made items that it may have taken weeks or even months to produce, will never fetch a decent price. But such is reality.

And, to boot, if you are the type, who cannot visit a flea market without coming home with a 'bargain', it is a dangerous place to be. You might come home with more than you brought there to sell.

So my advice is to give your stuff away. It will make both you and the receivers happy.

Do you ever finish a clean-out?

Yes, you do! It becomes a sport, a competition with yourself not to buy anything you don't need. You get to a point, when you buy only replacements for things that are broken, outdated or worn out. This is the result of owning only things you really appreciate and/or need.

WIPE YOUR SLATE!

Maintenance after a clean-out

So what do you do, when you have finished your clean out, in order to prevent it from starting all over again?

New Purchases

During this whole process you will have gone through so many questions about why you bought all the things you did, that it will change your buying habits. But situations will occur when all the old feelings pop up, and then you should ask yourself:

Did I spot this thing, because I need it?

Do I need to replace the old 'one'?

Are there any advantages to buying a new 'one'?

Do I really need to buy it this very minute, or can it wait?

Do I have room for it?

The answer to each question should be a clear yes, otherwise it is a no. So wait! The world won't run out of things, and tomorrow there will be a new and better bargain.

Bargains

We get a lot of flyers, emails, or watch TV ads offering bargains. There are

Time limited offers – not true. There will always be another

While stock lasts ... – there is always somebody with more

Everything has to go – yes, but you are not the person who is required to store it

Close out sales – just like any other sale. It will happen again.

Don't get fooled by those. There will always be new bargains – of all kinds.

General maintenance

Put things in their place
When you have the thing in your hand, put it in it's place. It sounds so boring, but don't give it a second thought. Just do it! That takes less time than running around looking for it next time you are going to use it.

Throw out
Broken things should be tossed immediately, and new replaces old. So if you buy a replacement, the old thing goes. Think: Out!

Once a year

On the anniversaries of your clean-out, you should go through all your things exactly like you did the first time. It will take less time, and over time there will be less and less to go through, because

you have only kept the good, useful things, haven't you?

WIPE YOUR SLATE!

A case study

I have previously mentioned a client whose story I will tell here, but the words are his, not mine, and they show clearly, how important it is to do a job like this yourself. He discovered, how he ended up in a situation in which he had gathered 88 moving boxes plus a lot of miscellaneous stuff in his basement. It appeared to be boxes with material in total order, but it was actually boxes, my client had just packed, when he felt that he had too much stuff taking up space in his apartment. So everything was packed very neatly in nice plastic boxes – without any filing system at all. But he had realized that it didn't work for him to have this big collection of boxes filled with papers and belongings. He got irritated when he couldn't find things, and he was aware that everything – no matter how well packed – got ruined by sitting down there in the basement. His wish was to sort with firm hand.

He contacted a storage company and rented two storage rooms facing each other, and he kept them for 2 weeks. We needed the time as well as the space. It is a good idea to remove everything, because then, dealing with each and every item becomes unavoidable. His intention was to hold everything in his hands, look at it, decide what to do with it – and then do it.

Our plan was to perform a preliminary sorting to get the feel of the job, and then proceed to a detailed sorting.

Every night, after having finished for the day, I interviewed, and as you will see, the process wasn't easy for him. His experience follows here.

Day 1

Me: *How do you feel now that day one of your clean-out has ended?*

My client: *I have a feeling of lots of lost work (the work he had stored in boxes). Maybe also wasted potential in the form of ideas and projects I never took the time to explore.*

Throwing out is not an entirely positive feeling. I feel as if I have been a guarantor, a custodian, a librarian, a protector of things (read: books and magazines), which has brought happiness or of things which I think were important, and will continue to be important. When you have put so much energy into a collection (IT- and music magazines) and you have a complete set of everything published from one point to another, some of the history will be wasted, when you let it go. A piece of history will vanish.

Me: *Do you feel that you are throwing away your own time?*

My client: *Yes, that too. What has brought me to this point is that I have acknowledged that there is a mismatch between how much I get in, and how much I throw out, and I have been like this all my life, so now I have to do it.*

Day 2

After 5½ hours of work and sorting some really 'tough' boxes that evoked childhood and teenage memories, my client was emotionally exhausted. This was not just like cleaning drain pipes. He had gone through something very personal, and this is one of the main reasons people don't even get started on cleaning out. You have to go through things you had put behind you.

Me: *When you go through your things now, I have noticed that you freeze, when the custodian is surfacing. What would you have done differently, if you had known that you were going to end up, where you are today?*

My client: *Actually I don't know. But I have realized that there is nothing called 'saving for later'. Everything I have put aside all these years, is the reason that I am now standing with my head buried in boxes. For example, the feeling of "this thing will be cool to have some time in the future". No, damn it, it is now that counts! All my small inventions, that I have made raw drafts for have actually been perfected by somebody later on. So I should have taken action, when the idea came to me. The lesson is not to wait to activate the idea later. It should be done now, or not at all. Projects should not be postponed. The one who hides things for later ... is standing with his head in boxes later.*

Would I have done it differently today? Yes, I would. Especially since I have seen this in- and outflow of things. From now on, logically I have to throw out just as much as I bring in. And I have discovered that it is not just a question of things. It is also a question of papers, notes, letters, cards, or the paper I wrote in school.

Everybody's an expert on cleaning out, but when it comes right down to it, you cannot do it yourself. You have to have help. You don't know how to do it, practically or physically.

Day 3

My client: *It has been a good day. I have thrown out something, which has made my inner archivist cry like a baby, but on the other hand – what would I use it for?*

Me: *You have not really reacted to the 'difficult' boxes today. How come? Yesterday you were almost ready to pass out, when you saw those boxes. Today you just started, and it is running real smoothly.*

My client: *Actually, I think it is more difficult today. The inner fight is the same, but I have been through it now, and I know how it ends, so I don't have to make the same considerations again. The result is the same. I see clearly that what I do, does not work. I will not get it done by myself, and I don't have endless basement rooms. I don't want endless basement rooms! What is important is not what was there. It is all about what is there now, and what affects tomorrow. Not what happened yesterday. So that impulse doesn't work. It is not healthy, because you get nowhere. It is also disgusting, because all the things perish. Things that are actually worth something, covered with things of no value, and everything becomes dirty, mouldy, and dusty.*

Am I happy about this? (the clean out) Yes, d... it, I am glad, and it is a victory every time a box is empty. And I feel a bit grrr (roaring sound) every time I fill one again (with the stuff to keep), even though they are the boxes, where all the good useful stuff is going to 'live'.

Me: *So afterwards you are going to take on another persona different from the archivist? Who is he going to be?*

My client: *He has to be a good organizer.*

Day 4

It is a 7:45 pm – we have worked for seven and a half hours.

My client: *It has been a really good day. We have started on the last half of the boxes, 44 units. But it has alternated between being very difficult, and very easy boxes. The hardest thing has been all my university papers. Not least because it is so far from what I am doing today. I have been thinking about this, why it has been so difficult, but it is probably because I worked so hard with these things, and now it only exists in these boxes. I haven't built anything on all that knowledge. Five years of work is reduced to these boxes here. Of course, it is like this for everybody who attends university, but for me it is a bit more, because I don't use any of it today.*

Me: *You changed to a totally different professional path?*

My client: *Yes, I did. But it doesn't change the fact that the projects I have in these boxes are difficult to say goodbye to, because I am actually rather proud of having been able to do this once, and I cannot do it anymore. I have nobody to show them to and share them with, so all I can do is pull out a couple of papers and look at them. But there is some pride in it.*

That is one side of all this, but now it is as if the clean out has accelerated a bit, because it has become routine. My biggest fear is actually that I might end up with too many boxes left anyway, and I have already heard the comment from you that I cannot have it all in my basement, the way I planned. We have to deal with that, and I hope that I can imagine, how it is going to look later, and where the problem actually is. The preliminary sorting is done, and that is a real great feeling, but I think it can become far better.

Me: *If you were to summarize the day, how was it? Harder, better, different?*

My client: *The start was really hard, but I am really, really relieved, because everything has been out in the open now.*

Day 5

My client: *It is really nice that there are no surprises left. We have looked through everything. Nothing to make me say: "Oh no, this will be difficult". I have seen everything, which means that I have a first hand impression of the worst areas that will need a lot of action. I have a general idea of the things, the mess, which now isn't that much of a mess anymore. It has changed from an unknown mess to a known amount of stuff, which has to be prioritized, sorted and organized – and sorted again.*

Day 6

My client: *It is late. We have just moved everything onto the trailer that is going to recycling. First load: 22 big moving boxes. It is a big victory. This is the part I have been looking forward to. The part where the scrap has been sorted away. Now it is gone.*

Last night when I got home, I was so tired. It really drains you. You are not only physically tired. You are emotionally tired. To go through every bit of your childhood to early youth and up until 2 years ago. It is just difficult. But there are 22 boxes on the trailer, and more will come. Boxes which will go to second hand stores and charity. So half of the things are gone now. With the order we have achieved now, we could stop the show and say: Good result. It is a giant step. But it can get better. In my eyes, we are only half way. I want to move on.

Me: *You have used the words opting out*

My client: *That's right. It is about opting out. Today we work with thousands of things, professional titles blend together, you are your own master, managing your own job. My point is that the identity you involuntarily create with what you make, has become much broader than before. So there is also a lot of identity in the basement.*

There are two things which for me are difficult, and I have to be very aware of them. I am, as I said 'The Guardian of Things'. I have been much too good at getting hold of these 'really-nice-to-own' things, and secondly, the other things which have been identity creators, the 'oh-I-cannot-loose-these' things, because they were related to people I care/cared about. I know that I don't hurt anybody, when I throw a clay figurine out. But tell that to the other side of my brain, which says exactly the opposite. I know that this old book is really disgusting and mouldy. That doesn't prevent me from thinking it is absolutely fantastic, because it once was, but of course I have to let it go. These are the most difficult variants. I have started to recognize the problem, but it doesn't make the process any less difficult. I am never going to have another nice figurine inside my house. No more 'this is really nice' things.

Day 7

My client: *Today was the day after the big preliminary sorting, and it was fantastic to get rid of a trailer filled with all kinds of things. How I feel right now? Right now I am just tired. Physically tired. I feel spent.*

We called my wife in to sort her own and our mutual belongings, and it was impressive, how easily she did that with yes, yes, yes, no, maybe to very few things, otherwise they were all clear no and no – proceed. Very impressive to watch.

Regarding all the useful things, I actually feel really good about giving them away to charity. I like the thought that they will come to use, instead of selling them at ridiculous prices – not to mention the difficulty involved with that. I prefer giving them away. The things will be put to use again and can hopefully create a bit of joy. If some kids can play with something that I once thought was cool, I will feel really good about that.

Day 8

My client: *The trailer has been a great success, but I still have about 30 boxes left, and that scares me a bit. I aimed at 10, but I don't think I will get there. I would like to get closer.*

Me: *I have to make a comment here. The plastic boxes you have chosen for storing things in now, are quite a lot smaller than the moving boxes, because you wanted them to be easy to handle in the basement, and you have computer equipment that has to occupy a box each. You also have a lot of tools that it would be silly to throw away.*

My client: *Of course, that's right! – and the noise is gone. What really made it for me was the preliminary sorting. And that the stuff for charity is gone. The rest is manageable. That is nice. It makes everything more pragmatic.*

I have seven boxes with comics! That is probably what takes up most space. It is so good now that I can see, how much it is. I have so many boxes with this, and so many boxes with that. I can see that in my head. It is so good to be able to say that in this box I can find these items, and that they aren't spread all over 15 boxes. That's a big thing! That is the dream scenario for the shape of the end result.

Day 9

My client: *Today we have worked in the basement, where all the sorted boxes are going back, and we found some very good solutions. There were actually a few things left there, and a lot of those are gone too. Now I am in this phase of throwing out, I can really differentiate good from bad. I have become so much better at distinguishing between what just has to go, and what is genuine. The unique things. The practical ones. A garden table is practical. A sleeping bag is practical. You would have to go out and buy those again, if you didn't already have them. But that doesn't mean I need 15 sleeping bags.*

Now there is an empty wall for all the boxes that are coming back. That is really nice. I will also have the dream fulfilled about being able to see everything at a glance – and get to them without any problems. There is room for 24 boxes, which is a quarter of what was there before. The boxes are smaller and more manageable, so it is probably something like 12 – 15 moving boxes.

Me: *Less than an hour ago you said that it might be possible to boil it down to fewer than these boxes?*

My client: *Yes, definitely! Now I can taste blood! There is a possibility of squeezing the number of boxes even more. I am a bit limited by the size of boxes though, since I chose such small ones. That makes the number a bit higher than I wanted. Clearly easier to handle, but irritating nevertheless.*

Day 10

The day before the last day! We have been here for 9 hours and 55 minutes. My client has really tasted blood!

Me: *We thought that this would become easier, and now – an entirely voluntary action – you have started a very detailed sorting!*

My client: *Well, this is actually where I feel that is necessary, because there will not be 'another time' to do it. We have fought the big battles, and now it is all the small things. I am down to wanting to close this box, but it still contains too much, so I have to sort this stupid box again. It takes time. I would really like to hit the wanted number of boxes. It would have been 9 boxes of the 88, but maybe that was unrealistic. Especially considering that I have a comics collection in 7 boxes and a lot of music and technical equipment. My tools have to be reconsidered.*

Me: *If one day you are going to use something in a box, do you think that you will then take the opportunity to sort it down to even less, while you are there anyway?*

My client: *I am quite sure that I will! The lesson yesterday going through my Christmas box! OK, yes, maybe the Christmas Hulk wasn't the coolest decoration.*

It has been a day of details, but we couldn't have done without it.

Me: *I feel like making a comment. You have cleared out 33 units for recycling at approxmately 7-8 kg each. This means that you have disposed of around 240-260 kgs. And that is only for recycling! That is a lot! And we are not even including what is going to charity. This really is a remarkable result!*

Day 11 – Last Day

My client: *I feel good. I just have to digest, what has happened. Now I will experience all the advantages. Due to my hoarder instinct I have had an inner fight, every time I removed anything. So it is a relief. And* *now it is done. It is all in the basement, and it is an impressive line up.*

How I feel? I have to learn how I feel. I have to start dealing with clutter another way. I have to make up my mind immediately. I just noticed a couple of stacks of paper on the desk at home that I have to do someting about. The kind of stacks I used to think –'arrrgh!' about, and then put in a box, so the place would look nice again. I actually like it when my home looks nice. But I have to stop putting things in boxes for 'dealing' with later. Because 'later' will, as mentioned before, end up with me struggling in a basement room. I have learned to recognise the habits. I can see the system.

Me: *Is there a victory in this?*

My client: *I wish that I could say 'Yeah! Victory!', and I probably will at some point, but not right now. Right now it is 'Yeah! Done!', and the boxes I have now contain things of value to me. Something useful.*

Me: *You have always had a neat home, and now it has spread to your basement. So there is no more clutter in your life.*

My client: *Yes, that's true. Clearly, this clean out has strengthened my willpower to withstand bringing new things into the apartment. Because that is the way I have to tackle it. Once it is there, I have to fight with the feeling of having to preserve it at any price. I have learned that I have an irrational feeling in me that makes me incredibly good at taking the easy way out and just stack things on top of each other. Only the fact that I am an aesthete has prevented me from becoming an all out hoarder. Only self criticism has kept this from happening. But I clearly have a hoarder gene.*

There is a good feeling about having boiled everything down. You don't need 50 litres of diluent belongings . Maybe just a little bit of concentrate would be better. To crystallize things, so only the best crystals are left.

Me: *Do you have more to say?*

My client: *Yes, thank you. It has been a big thing for me. I have a life now, where everything underneath me (in the basement) isn't a garbage dump anymore, and I have uncovered a mechanism to keep it that way.*

WIPE YOUR SLATE!

Aftermath

My client thought it could be fun to take the interviewer's part and switch roles. He wanted to ask me some questions, and it was a fun experience. Something new always crops up when a new person asks good questions:

Client: *I am the archivist/the custodian/the librarian/the guardian/the collector for the conservation of things. Who are you?*

Me: *I am the simplifier.*

Client: *You are now! But you haven't always been that, have you?*

Me: *Yes, it has always been in me. But I was raised to believe that owning many things was good.*

Client: *So that is where the problem started. What is the core of your problem?*

Me: *Guilty conscience. I didn't want to hurt anybody, so I didn't start cleaning up until my mid 40s.*

Client: You were the pleaser. Can you describe it in more detail? Did you discover this slowly?

Me: *I remember it as being hit by a bomb. But I have some childhood memories about wanting to have less (see the chapter ' A childhood Memory'). If I had had less, I am quite sure that I would have appreciated my possessions more, so I have been a camouflaged minimalist all my lift. I was in the closet.*

Client: So now the reaction is that you want the opposite. You want to be a minimalist, because it is the only way that you can find out, who you are.

Me: *Yes, but maybe that isn't all. I find diffusion difficult. I don't appreciate a collection of 500 units of some kind. It is too noisy. I like a collection of 2 items.*

Client: You have become an anti-collector.

Me: *If you have other people's values forced upon you, you react to the pressure. I was raised as a collector, and that 'a lot' is good, so I reacted, as you said, by becoming an anti-collector. To find myself I had to cross the street. I have thought the thought: If my home burned down, and everything living was saved — of course — what would be the first thing I would do?*

Client: Interestingly, that it is a very clear reaction. You don't think about what you would save, but that you are 'burning down your house'. You are cleaning out.

Me: *I have actually seen two families among my friends, who lost everything in fires, so these thoughts come automatically.*

Client: It has really gotten to you. In your head you destroy everything that isn't you, and start over. Then, nobody can impose anything upon you. Then you can find yourself.

Me: *I have finished that thought! and you know what my biggest fear is? That I would never again buy anything. That I would live in my bed with an orange crate for 'all' my things.*

Client: Now Freud or Jung is happy (laughter). You want as little as possible, because your surroundings have imposed so much on you.

Me: *Yes, but in return, I demand that all my belongings be personal, and good quality.*

Client: Of course. The things that express who you are, must be the best.

Me: *At least they have to be personal. Not necessarily the most expensive.*

Here the interview between the collector/the guardian and the simplifyer/closet minimalist ended.

WIPE YOUR SLATE!

So far - so good

So – now you have cleaned up in your 'physical' world.

Well, maybe not yet.

But I have to take this a bit further anyway. Because when I was done with my home and my belongings, I had such an excess of energy, that I started looking at other sides of my life which didn't quite work, and my finances were definitely something worth looking at.

Because of my changed surroundings, I had changed my purchasing habits. I didn't buy little cute or decorative items, and I didn't buy clothes which didn't fit with the rest of my wardrobe, but I still found it difficult to define how I actually spent my money.

So I had to dig in again, and this time it was a lot easier. I knew the way.

WIPE YOUR SLATE!

Finances

I have to start with a very indiscreet question:

Is it actually your own money you are spending?

Because if you are one of the many, who spend more than you earn, I can tell you that keeping your finances in order is the easiest thing in the world!

You need 3 nails on the wall!

On nail no. 1 – you hang your pay
slip

On nail no. 2 – you hang a list of
your expenses

On nail no. 3 – pay minus
expenses = the
amount you can
spend as you wish
until next pay day!!

It is that simple!

The method is bullet proof, and will show you quite clearly that you cannot live in a water front castle if your income is only slightly higher than when you were in high school.

Joking aside, most of us wouldn't mind having more money. Money gives freedom and security. But I don't think that is the whole truth. To be Scrooge McDuck has no value in itself. He is lying on top of his money in this money tank, and rewards no one, not even himself. If that makes him happy it's OK with me. I believe that money has an energy. If I am saving without a goal, there will be no energy in my money, but there will be, if I have a goal. The money I save will go to something that I want and/or need.

The dream is often about having enough. But what is enough? For me, it is having sufficient for my everyday life, for a holiday, gifts, clothes etc. On an ordinary salary, that is quite manageable. I don't need more than that. Have I ever dreamt about the mansion by the sea, the Mercedes in the garage, or the boat at the yacht club? No I haven't, because I don't want to be enslaved by having to take care of many things.

The smart reader will now comment:

But if you were rich, you could have people taking care of them!

Yes, but then I would have to take care of the people taking care of my things. I prefer having the freedom to spend my money on seeing new things and places, and meeting new people.

The smart reader: Yes, but you could still do that. And I could, but – and here is something very important to me – if I were so rich that I could do exactly what I wanted, I wouldn't experience the joy of anticipation! The joy of working and saving for something, while I can examine if it is something that will really make me happy. Sentimental romantic? Some might think so, but the experience described below turned the picture of wealth and financial freedom upside down in my head – and it is one of the stories making my best friend laugh hysterically while saying ..." like the time with your bracelet ...":

Some years ago I fell in love with a very beautiful gold bracelet. It was quite expensive – to put it mildly – but I had to have it. I started a savings account, and I was really striving to buy everything else as cheaply as possible whenever possible. I avoided impulse purchases, so I saved every penny I could

– except when it came to food and necessities for the family. When I got close to the goal – almost 3 year later! – I went to the store to try it on. In that very moment with the bracelet on my wrist – the bracelet for which I had been saving for almost 3 years! –I knew that I didn't want it anymore. I clearly wanted it, when this quest started, but in time, the goal became saving money!

I didn't buy it, and I was very happy on my way home. It wasn't an anticlimax at all, because it was one of the best financial experiences I have ever had. It was precisely at that point that I realized I could do and have whatever I wanted – if I would pay the price. I had paid the price, namely that I had shown the stamina not to buy unimportant stuff for myself for a very long time. I had reached the finish line. I did it.

The bonus included in this experience was learning that the road toward a goal isn't boring, but actually quite exciting in a sporty kind of way. It was fun chasing it, and it was even more fun to get there, even though I later realized that I had changed course along the way without changing the goal. I changed course at the last minute, so I taught myself to look up from the track to see if I am going in the right direction, or if my wishes and needs have changed.

My son and I went to Paris for a week, and when I came home, there was still money in my account. I also found that I much prefer having enjoyable experiences with the people I love rather than chasing things.

Some considerations

In Denmark we have a TV channel running shows about people in financial difficulties. Two experts try to solve their problems, and make budgets for them. I have noticed an identical pattern for almost all the households. The couples, who bought houses and redecorated, have similar looking homes. Everything in the house is bought 'within a week', it seems. So in 15 years all the homes will look like 15 years old homes. The things on the wall, the furniture, nothing personal, no fantasy. Expensive without being of lasting quality. And very often the reason these people are so deeply in debt. What is so wrong with starting out small, and gathering things little by little? But no, the attitude is: We have bought a house and spent a huge amount of money redecorating the kitchen, so let us spend another huge amount on a new bathroom, AND buy new furniture for the whole house at the same time and bury ourselves in even bigger debt. To be so unrealistic after having just bought a house, without knowing anything about house ownership. That is financial stupidity!

Maybe the bank's information was that you can afford it – but the bank is in business to lend money and collect interest, so it is in your best interest to dig into it and do the math yourself.

Some years ago I was looking at an apartment I wanted to buy. I went to the bank, and they made a budget for me, which showed that I could easily afford to buy it. No problems at all, the bank lady said, after having entered my financial details into the form.

When I got home, I sat down and looked at it. Amounts for light, insurance, heat etc. were estimated correctly. But there was no column for maintenance of the apartment, nor for car repairs, dentist, holidays, fitness, clothes and shoes, or any kind of social life. In other words there were no expenses included for anything more than a roof over my head. None of the things I appreciate, and that make me feel I get something out of my salary, were included.

I redid the budget myself. I increased the amount for heat, because it was lower than for the smaller apartment I was living in. Then I added estimated amounts for the things mentioned above. I also added some for a savings account for unexpected expenses or large purchases. On top of all this I added expenses for moving and all the little bits, bobs, and nails you have to buy when you move, as well as for making repairs to the apartment I was leaving.

The result yelled out loud, that I could not afford the apartment, if I wanted to live the kind of life that suited me. So I stayed, where I was.

To be fair about it: it wasn't the bank lady's responsibility. **it was mine**. So after re-budgeting, I realized I would actually need to borrow quite a lot more than calculated from the start. If I had bought the apartment, I would have ended up having to eat for a month for an amount corresponding to what I would normally spend in a week – a very strict regime. There was no flexibility in that budget, and no allowance for anything unexpected. It was a real good exercise.

A loan is a loan no matter what. It will cost you one way or another. High interest, or interest free for a period (sometimes available), the banks and other lenders do not give anything away. For every loan from a bank, credit company or any other place, you increase your debt. It shouldn't be necessary to write it, but it is! You are tied to it. When you have borrowed 100,000 of whatever kind of currency, you are 100,000 in debt.

Sometimes I wonder why people want to own their own house. In earlier times it was quite understandable. It was an investment, and the system worked so that at some point in time the mortgage would be paid off. Then you had an asset, and would only have to pay for maintenance and regular expenses when you got older.

The situation is different today. People are moving around more to find work, so a house can now be an obstacle, if you cannot sell it, or if you have to sell at a big loss. So it can be risky business to buy, if you don't know whether you will be staying forever.

Am I in favour of renting? I am neutral. I just think that you have to take into consideration what kind of life you live/want to live, and not everybody is suited for having either a house or an apartment. Not everybody can live with wall to wall neighbours, and not everybody thinks gardening is fun.

I don't want the responsibility of having to think about the plumbing or the new furnace or a leaking roof. I am not that handy, and there are things I would rather spend my time on, so I would have to pay my way out of any repairs. Of course, there may be a certain charm in working in your own garden, having a barbeque and making the lawn look nice. I just prefer to go down to the lawn mown by the maintenance crew and have a barbeque with the other tenants on the shared grill.

Apartment or house is not actually the primary question. Ask yourself how you want to live, and let that make the decision for you. There are pros and cons either way. One is not better than the other. They are just two different ways to live.

But it is a fact that way too many people buy expensive houses without having a clue about all the financial obligations involved, or even without having consulted specialists who know the traps and have no interest in the money side of it. So financial advice and a professional home inspection will always be money saved in the long run. Choose independent advice.

If you want the mansion at the beach, and you cannot afford it now, you have to do something about it. Because it is not free. You have to earn more money. That is what it is all about. You have to be ready to pay the price and make the effort to get what you want. Taking out endless loans is irresponsible, so if you are not ready to do that, you will have to make do with what you already have. Right! I'm not kidding. Don't live above your means and think that somebody will come and pick you up when it goes wrong, because that will not happen. It is as simple as that.

You should never make your home into something temporary. It only creates the need for something 'more'. If you live in a place, which is not exactly what you would want, you have to make the best of what you have now. Just because it isn't your dream scenario, doesn't mean you can't make it nice. You can build up a base of good things that you can bring with you, if or when you have the option of moving somewhere else. You should make your best efforts to live as comfortably and well functioning as possible. A home is not the walls around you. It is what you put between those walls – mentally and physically.

Test if you can afford your dream house

If you walk around dreaming about buying a house or a condo, you can easily test, if you can afford it:

1 Find a house similar to the house you are dreaming about. It should be exactly the neighbourhood, the size etc. that you want. Everything has to be right. Contact a real estate agent and get the facts and the costs concerning the place.

2 Make an estimate of monthly costs of living there, and remember to include any and all kinds of taxes, renovations, insurance, maintenance, heating, water etc. in the budget.

3 Now take the difference between your current equivalent monthly expenses and the amount you would have to pay, if you already lived in your dream house, and put that amount in the bank every month for a year.

If you can afford that – saving this amount – you can afford your dream house! You now have a totally realistic picture of what you would have to spend on all new expenses, and at the same time you have started a savings account, which you – if you are really smart – continue adding to until you have the money for the down payment and all the expenses connected with the purchase. That's it!

You can start looking into you everyday spending to get an even better understanding of your finances.

Collect all receipts for a couple of months and put them in a box. I am talking about ALL receipts, including the little necklace, the burger, the chocolate milk and the new hub caps for the car. Everybody with access to the account should do this. After 2-3 months take all the receipts and divide them into different categories, for example:

groceries, house cleaning products;

clothes;

personal 'maintenance'
(hairdresser, cosmetics, aftershave, etc.);

transportation;

magazines, books;

gifts;

pleasures (movies, lunches, lattes etc.);

miscellaneous.

If the miscellaneous pile gets too tall, it is probably because you have a 'hidden' habit, which isn't included in the categories mentioned above, but I am sure that you can spot it, when you go through all the receipts in this pile, and then you will have to add a new category.

All these expenses are the ones NOT going into the budget, I talked about before – the fixed expenses. Rent, heating, insurance etc.

Now add up the totals for each category and you will see where the biggest load lies. It will become very obvious if there is a hidden special expense. For example, a bottle of red wine twice a week will turn into quite a substantial amount for the year. And it doesn't even have to be high quality wine at that.

Fun and games

Vacations are wonderful, but going abroad to some exotic place once or several times a year is not one of the basic human rights.

Vacations may be mandated by labour laws, but traveling isn't

A lot of people seem to think it is, and some are even prepared to go into debt to do it. They take a loan to go on vacation. They borrow money to go away! It is a really, really bad idea, because how much fun is it to pay for something that is over? And gone! You cannot see it anymore, and after a few days, you cannot even feel it. Vacations are only momentary pleasures. Yes, you can remember good vacations, but if you borrowed the money for them, it might cast a shadow on the fun, once they are over.

Some will claim that it is good to get away from home! To see and experience something new. This is somewhat true, but 'away' is mostly a question about doing something different, and you don't have to fly thousands of miles to do that. In all honesty, an unpaid for vacation can actually be quite stressing – when it is waiting for you at home as a new debt.

Having your holidays at home – a staycation – is not always cheaper than going abroad. Actually, when you are at home, going out might cost you the same, or more, when it comes to food, although there are not many 'cheap' countries anymore. However, when you travel, you often act on impulse and buy things, even though later you have not the slightest clue why you bought them, and you would definitely never have bought them while at home. We know what things cost, when we are 'at home', so there are no surprises, and if you go to the beach, you can bring your own food. A lot of money are saved, and the kids will have the food, they like. For children, vacation is often about the time they spend together with their (hopefully unstressed) parents, so it is not necessarily about 'being away'.

Weddings are often financed through credit cards and loans. These celebrations are often excessively expensive – but why? Because a wedding is a 'once-in-a-lifetime' event? Well, maybe for approximately half of us, to be quite cynical about it. The focus is on expensive details, and 'expensive' has never, ever been essential for a good party. Maybe for an impressive party, but not for a good one, because that comes from the heart, not from the wallet. You can arrange until hell freezes over, but you cannot buy the party mood. No fancy decorations can either. The mere thought that anyone would be ready to spend on a wedding party an amount equivalent to a down payment on a house is totally crazy. No arguments can justify this.

A wedding should be a question more about saying yes to each other, than about feeding 100 people 6 courses and a big cake – or about a dress worn only once. I am definitely not unromantic, but if the romance is going to suffer afterwards in everyday life because of the debt load, I think I would choose a more 'humble' wedding on the day and peace in everyday life afterwards. It is no secret that a lot of arguments and quarrelling in marriages are about money.

You could choose a whole different approach and ask your friends to help make a wedding. Ask family and friends if there is somebody who knows somebody who can make a wedding bouquet, who knows about a good venue, and who might have a nice wedding dress or can make one, and who knows a good chef. A young couple I know, who had moved in together and had everything they needed in their home already, sent out invitations saying that they didn't want presents. They wanted to see everybody they cared about on their special day, and asked for presents in the form of other kinds of contributions. It was a great success. Three of the guests performed a song written by the groom for the bride in the church. One girl was a pastry maker. She made the wedding cake, and two couples paid for the ingredients. Four guys played and sang during the reception, and two amateur photographers covered the wedding with their cameras all day. Some took care of transportation from the reception to the wedding dinner, one guest had a special car, which became the ride for the bride to the church, and so on, and so on. Everybody contributed with what they could do, and it was the greatest party ever.

So in summary: Don't borrow money for 'events'. The aftermath is not worth it. When it is over, you have hopefully had a great day, which would have been so much better, if you didn't have to start paying off the debt, once the fun was over, and you were back to everyday life. So make a sport of it. Make a financially manageable plan, stick to it, and enjoy the ride! But remember to adjust the course along the way! Don't spend more than you earn. You sleep a lot better with fewer things than with a lot of things, which aren't actually yours!

> "We act as though comfort and luxury
> were chief requirements of life,
> when all that we need to
> make us really happy
> is something to be
> enthusiastic about".
>
> – Charles Kingsley

WIPE YOUR SLATE!

Financial maintenance

Monthly

It is not a lot of work, but it gives so much peace! So do it! All you need are 3 'nails'/accounts:

1. A Budget Account, from which all your fixed expenses are paid. The expenses you have no choice but to pay. Rent, heating, school, insurance, petrol, etc. Calculate a monthly estimate covering these expenses, and make the bank transfer the money automatically.

2. A Savings Account. No matter how little you can save, it is a good idea to have a small buffer for unforeseen expenses. Also to be transferred automatically by your bank.

3. Then your are left with the money
you can spend as you wish, and this is
the account connected to your credit
(you only need one!) or debit card.
This is the amount which will
cover all expenses other than the fixed
ones. All your spending throughout the
month.

If you always have an overdraft on that third account, figure out
why (see earlier chapter), and make a plan to reduce and/or
eliminate it.

Don't juggle between your accounts. By that I mean: never move
money from one account to another. If you move money from
the budget account to cover something else, you will end up
missing that amount the following month, and then your will have
an overdraft in that account too.

So the only thing you have to do is the monthly check. When you
get the hang of it, it will take at the most 20 minutes, and then you
will not have to look at it until the following month – provided you
spend only the amount in your credit card account every month.

To get a clear picture of what funds will be available after fixed
expenses are taken care of, produce a budget form with 14
columns – one for descriptive details, one for each month (12),
and one for the total year. In the first column list separately Income
and Expenses, with subcategories for each. Suggested details are
listed below, and if required, other items can be added. Enter
definite and/or estimated amounts for each category for each
month, and totals for the year in the final column. Total expenses
must go into the budget account, a decided upon amount into the

savings account, and hopefully there will still be some money left from the total income amount, which can be spent as you see fit.

Annually
Once a year you will have to make a new budget to see if anything has changed. Maybe you have new or fewer expenses, so make corrections, but as things usually don't get cheaper, you should increase each expense item by a couple of percent, and then you will be covered. If you plan on a large purchase, then increase the amount going to the savings account, so it is clearly visible to you that you are saving for it.

Don't ever disregard financial problems. Seek advise ASAP.

Do something about it before it does you in.

It may not be easy, but it is very, very important that you are in **control** of your money. No matter if you have a lot or very little. It provides **the ultimate calm**.

Income

		Jan	Feb	...	Dec	Total
Wages and Salary	Pensions/ Annuities					
Retirement Income	Social Security					
	Child Support					
Other income						
Other income:	Unemployment Compensation					
Investment income						
TOTAL						

This spreadsheet is available on my web site www.wipeyourslate.com.

Expenses

		Jan	Feb	...	Dec	Total
Shelter	Rent/Mortgage payment					
	Maintenance/Renovation					
Bills	Electricity					
	Natural gas/oil					
	Water and sewer					
	Garbage and Recycle					
	Telephone					
	Cellular					
	Cable/Satellite TV					
	Online/Internet service					
Transportation	Car payments					
	Gasoline					
	Car maintenance					
	Parking					
	Public transit					
Food	Groceries					
	Dining out					
	Alcohol					
Insurance	Homeowner/Home contents					
	Automobile					
	Medical and Dental					
	Life					
Taxes	Income tax					
	Property tax					
Savings	Pension					
	Vacation					
	Children					
Miscellaneous	Leisure: Books/Magazines					
	Leisure: Cultural events					
	Leisure: Sporting events					
	Leisure: Gym membership					
	Gifts					
	Other					
TOTAL						

This spreadsheet is available on my web site www.wipeyourslate.com.

WIPE YOUR SLATE!

The end

If you have now decided to clean up and out in your home and your finances, what will that mean for you? I cannot know that, but I can tell you what it has meant for me:

Having cleaned out and started over with as clean a slate as possible has been enormously liberating. It turned a lot of things upside down. Once I reclaimed my freedom in my apartment, the need to clean up in my two basement rooms came very fast. The mess down there was like a debilitating noise. Like a roaring monster in the deep. Exactly like all my unfinished projects – until I killed them.

I got breathing space in my everyday life, so I didn't have a stack of duties always lying in front of me. The 'pleasure' of washing the floor under my bed was almost silly. I felt so good, it takes 2 minutes for me – I, who always hated washing floors! Because now I don't have to move 2 boxes, a vacuum cleaner and other stored away things. The boxes don't exist anymore, and the vacuum cleaner has it own space, where it is easy to get to. There is absolutely nothing under my bed anymore.

My girlfriends will not get DIY things for Christmas, and they will not get the homemade Christmas card either, but on the other hand, I am happy and relaxed. The need to do everything myself has been replaced with doing what I want to do, and doing it properly. I have recognized that I don't have unlimited amounts of time, and I make conscious decisions about how I will spend the time I do have.

It has also had other effects, which are just as important. I don't feel the same need for owning things anymore. I repeat:

I don't feel the same need for owning things anymore!

The world is filled with beautiful things, but just because I think they are beautiful, doesn't mean I need to have them. I can buy them, if I want, because I know that I can save for the things, I want. But my home is beautiful in my eyes, and it functions well for me, so I don't often feel the need for new stuff. I love books, but I don't need to have them all on my book shelf. I have set myself free from wanting EVERYTHING.

When I go shopping, I have a shopping list for my daily needs. I also have a list of things, which could be good to get for my wardrobe, and it has a permanent home in my purse, so if I feel tempted, I look at what I have fallen in love with, and if it isn't on my list, I don't buy. On the other hand, I can now afford to buy it, If by chance I see something, which is on the list.

There are a lot of theories about how long it takes to break a habit, and one of them says 21 days. So try that! When you are done with your cleaning project, wait for 21 days before you buy anything other than food.

Other things have happened later. Without really having given it much thought, I have gradually changed my home. I didn't realize this until recently, when I saw photos taken in my place after the clean up. I have disposed of several things, which, I later found out, I didn't really want to have around anyway. So I just moved the remaining furniture a little further apart, which gave more space. Without thinking about it, I had 'cut to the bone'. I need less and less – but what is left must be good! First class! Exactly what I want, and I will wait for it if necessary.

Because I am not a slave of my things

Because I have purchased quality things

Because I am difficult to tempt with things, and

Because I have, what I need – of good quality - and I don't need a lot.

Except good people in my life, and good experiences.

I haven't had more time. I have given myself more time.

There are so many people who are 'staging' their lives. They want to look a certain way, and they want to be perceived a certain way, but you can choose, if you want to live a life that is yours, or if you want to copycat others. It doesn't matter what you have. It matters what you do with what you have. You are in charge. The genuine way to live is what you choose for yourself.

When you **live** in a way that **feels comfortable**

When you have a **job** that makes you happy

When you **dress**, so it **suits** you and your life

When you **spend** the money that's yours (and **no more**)

When you **do** the things you really **want to do**

When you **live with** the **people you love**, and see people whose company you appreciate

And when you do it all **properly**.

Some people own a lot of things.
Others own good things.

Now I just want you to find out, what makes you happy, and to throw everything else overboard.

Bon voyage!

WIPE YOUR SLATE!

50 pieces of good advice

If you follow just **one** of these, your life will become easier:

1 Children's art work – find a special place for it and tell the child that when something new goes up, the old ones will be taken down and put in a box or binder (then you can sort it without the child participating). In other words, make it a tradition, so the child feels that it is a good ritual, and knows that you appreciate his/her talent

2 Collect all papers concerning all financial transactions in a binder, one for each year, and throw out the ones 5 years or older, excepting papers that must be kept 'forever'

3 All membership cards have their own place – f.ex. in your hallway in a drawer

4 Don't read flyers offering bargains

5 Cancel all subscriptions – especially magazine subscriptions. For the most part, you don't have the time to read them properly anyway

6 Divide all bills and receipts into categories: food, transportation, clothes, personal hygiene, medications, fun etc., and enter them into budget columns at month's end. It will show you where you can save money

7 Books, that you know you will never read again, should be given away to someone who will – read them, that is

8 Sort your clothes and your shoes at least once a year and give everything that doesn't fit to somebody who needs it

9 Never buy knick knacks for which you don't have a specific plan. Nobody needs knick knacks

10 Don't accept any hand-me-downs, unless it is something you really need

11 Use the things you have, if they work. The thermos from last year can still keep the coffee warm. You don't need a new one

12 Stop buying storage boxes. They make your home smaller and your clutter bigger

13 Don't put anything in your basement, attic or 'junk' room if you don't know what to do with it. Make somebody happy and give it away – or take it to be recycled

14 Buy groceries once a week

15 Only buy what's on your list

16 Know that there will always be another offer – if you should have missed a bargain

17 Know where its place will be in your home before buying something new

18 If you buy a replacement for something (a new iron, f.ex.) be sure to immediately throw away the old one

19 When you feel the urge to go shopping, buy a chocolate bar or a cookie instead

20 Having 2 of the same kind (of anything) it is not the same as starting a collection

21 Style yourself and your house for your own comfort, and forget about 'trends'

22 Stay away from flea markets, unless you are looking for a specific item, and then buy only that and nothing else

23 Don't buy anything for a new project, unless you have the time to complete it now

24 One person (adult) doesn't need more than 3 sets of bed linen

25 Go through your medicine cabinet and check expiry dates. Take the expired items to the pharmacy for proper disposal

26 Don't buy more food than you can eat

27 Throw out all grocery coupons – you don't need it all. Not even if it is cheap

28 Throw out more than 3 months old make-up and cosmetics

29 Never stick your fingers in a cream jar. It becomes a bacteria bomb. Use a spatula (you can get it at a cosmetics store)

30 Kill the concept 'miscellaneous' in your files. Miscellaneous is another word for clutter

31 Kill the concept 'must-have'. It is nonsense invented by marketing people

32 Clear out your kitchen cabinets, so you don't have to move 7 things in order to find what you need

33 You don't need 5 mixing bowls

34 Put things away before you go to bed. It takes 5 minutes. A cluttered house at the start of the day drains your energy

35 Save money for the bigger things, you want. It is very expensive to borrow money, and the joy of anticipation is very worthwhile

36 If you 'have to' take out a loan, only have one at a time (not 15 credit cards, all with charges, on the side)

37 Trust that you taste is OK. You don't have to change everything every season

38 Remove all stuff under your bed, and you will sleep better

39 It is OK to buy bargains only if it is something you normally buy anyway – unless it creates a space problem. As noted, new bargains will always pop up

40 Acknowledge that you don't need to own everything, even if you find whatever it is nice/impressive/fantastic

41 The less you own, the easier to keep a neat home

42 Collect bottles and newspapers/ magazines in a tote, so it is easy to take with you, when you leave home

43 Gather your bed linen in sets after laundry, and put sheet and duvet cover inside the pillow case. Then you don't have to look for matching sets

44 Never buy anything until you have checked that you don't already have something at home almost the same

45 Find out what all family members' expectations for a good holiday are. That way you can take action to make it enjoyable for everybody

46 Don't use a credit card to pay for vacations or parties. It is so annoying to pay for an experience that is long since gone

47 Wait to buy things which aren't necessities until the end of the month. If there is no money in the account, you cannot afford it

48 Keep a continually current wish list. Go through it once a month to find out if a wish was just a whimsy, or if you still want it (which you very well might not!)

49 Give away things you don't use, so they can benefit somebody else

50 Graffiti artist Banksy quote:
The best things in life are not things

WIPE YOUR SLATE!

My website
wipeyourslate.com

www.ingramcontent.com/pod-product-compliance
Lightning Source LLC
LaVergne TN
LVHW021449080426
835509LV00018B/2218